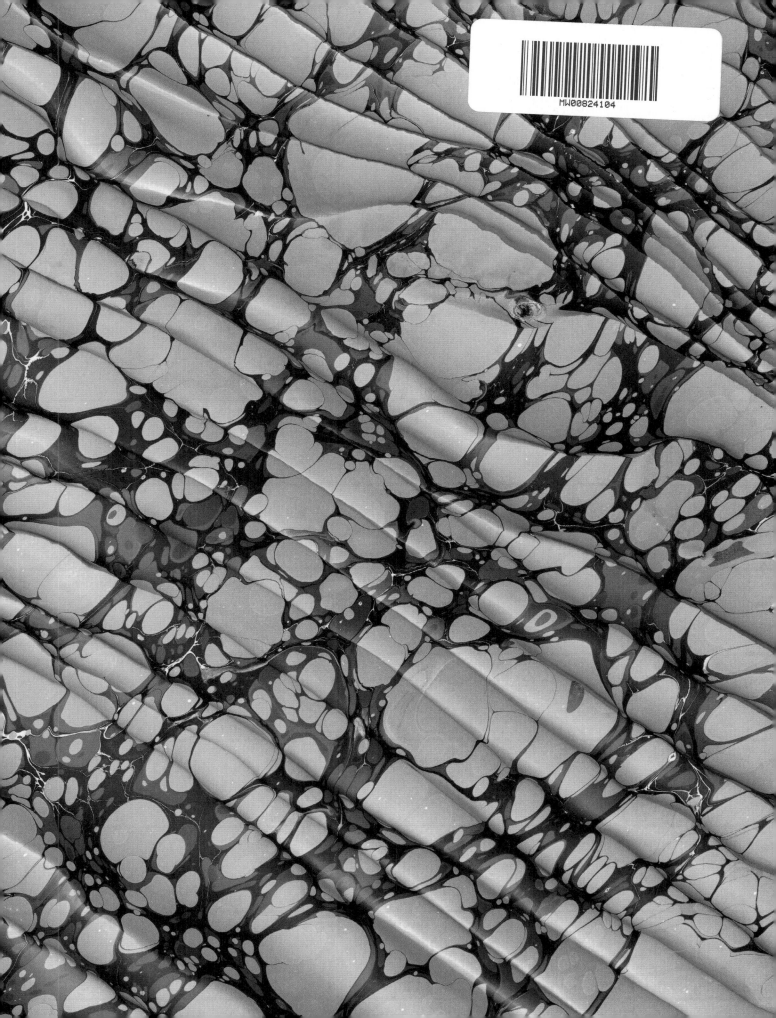

Halftracked Vehicles

of the German Army 1909-1945

Walter J. Spielberger

Schiffer Military History
Atglen, PA

The drawings in this book were kindly made available by Mr. Hilary Doyle, who is, like the author, a colleague of BELLONA Publication Ltd.

Our thanks go to BELLONA for giving permission to reproduce these drawings. They provide by far the most complete information on military vehicles inside and outside Germany.

Four-side drawings in 1/76 and 1/48 scales are available through specialist firms or directly from BELLONA Publications Ltd., Bridge Street, Hemel Hempstead, Herts, England, United Kingdom

Scale Drawings: Hilary L. Doyle
Color Illustrations: Uwe Feist
Photo credits:
Federal Archives/Military Archives (34), P. Chamberlain Collection (2), Hilary Doyle Collection (4), Uwe Feist Archives (28), Ford Motor Company (2), Private Hentschel (2), Prof. W. Hess (1), Robert J. Icks Collection (13), Kloeckner-Humboldt-Deutz AG (2), Kraus-Maffei AG (12), Adam Opel AG (3), Werner Oswald Archives (4), H. Schultetus (1), Walter J. Spielberger Archives (307), Bart Vanderveen (2), F. Wiener Collection (4).

Book translation by Dr. Edward Force, Central Connecticut State

Book Design by Ian Robertson.

Printed in China.
ISBN: 978-0-7643-2942-5

This book was originally published in German under the title
die Halbketten-Fahrzeuge des Deutschen Heeres 1909-1945 by Motorbuch Verlag

We are interested in hearing from authors with book ideas on related topics.

Published by Schiffer Publishing Ltd.
4880 Lower Valley Road
Atglen, PA 19310
Phone: (610) 593-1777
FAX: (610) 593-2002
E-mail: Info@schifferbooks.com.
Visit our web site at: www.schifferbooks.com
Please write for a free catalog.
This book may be purchased from the publisher.
Please include $3.95 postage.
Try your bookstore first.

In Europe, Schiffer books are distributed by:
Bushwood Books
6 Marksbury Avenue
Kew Gardens
Surrey TW9 4JF, England
Phone: 44 (0) 20 8392-8585
FAX: 44 (0) 20 8392-9876
E-mail: Info@bushwoodbooks.co.uk.
Visit our website at: www.bushwoodbooks.co.uk
Free postage in the UK. Europe: air mail at cost.
Try your bookstore first.

Contents

Foreword

Motor vehicles and terrains have been opposed to each other since the beginning of their development, a fact that has resulted in outstanding technical developments for many years. In off-road vehicles, solutions that went far beyond the limits of normal use had to be found, which almost always involved new technical territory.

For centuries, towing by animals was the only means of moving heavy burdens. It also determined the size classes of the equipment and weapons to be moved. The introduction of the steam engine brought a basic change. Despite that, even steam engines were usually limited to rails and roads.

When Holt introduced the first useful caterpillar tractor in America at the end of the 19th century, the possibility of using motorized towing vehicles off paved roads also opened up. The first half-tracked vehicles were built at that time. It was a long, difficult process of development that finally led to the halftrack towing vehicles of the German *Wehrmacht*. These vehicles formed the last step of the development that created outstanding military vehicles. Extraordinary towing performance on and off roads, high average speed, little wear on the road surfaces, and considerable soundlessness were attained there.

The present volume of the "Military Vehicles" book series offers what is now the most thorough assemblage of military halftrack vehicles. Laboriously built in technical terms, they were really just a burden in production and maintenance, despite the fulfilling of their tasks in the war years. The attempts to create less costly towing vehicles, with few exceptions, never progressed beyond the initial stages.

In addition, even at the beginning of their development, the creation of a variety of types was striven for, which could lead only to problems in serious cases. Yet no other army utilized halftrack vehicles in as great variety as the German Army. Documenting this development was part of our task.

Although these vehicles, as opposed to armored vehicles, were not always built under the same conditions of secrecy, only meager documentation of the beginning of their development existed. We hope, though, with this publication to have created the framework that will enable us to expand the developmental history further. For this, as always, the cooperation of many experts is necessary. We must therefore thank all of those who have taken part in this research for decades.

Once again, we recognize the help of Colonel Robert J. Icks, who greatly supported the expansion of the meager sources after the war's end. Dr. Fritz Wiener also played a decisive role in the work. We also think of Messrs. Uwe Feist, Peter Chamberlain, Dick Hunnicutt, Heinrich Scultetus, and Bart Vanderveen, who enhanced the total results again and again with added documentation and photographic material. Last but not least, we must mention Hilary L. Doyle, whose unique work brought new aspects of this development to light time after time, and without whose drawings the whole series of books would lack much of its contents.

This group of researchers hopes once again for numerous communications from readers, whom we thank above all for constructive criticism.

Walter J. Spielberger
Trieblach 9
A-9210 Poertschach z. W., Austria

The Development of German Halftrack Vehicles for Military Use

A. From 1890 to 1919

The first attempts to create usable tracked tractors for agricultural use were carried out in 1890 by the Stockton Wheel Company in California. To be able to control the steering of such vehicles, the first versions of these "Caterpillars" still had steerable wheels at the front. Thus, the first halftrack vehicles came to be. This principle was kept and developed further, and was viewed by other lands as a means of making load-carrying off-road vehicles.

This idea was taken up for the first time in Germany when the Daimler Motor Company in Berlin-Marienfelde developed a heavy towing vehicle with all-wheel drive in 1908-09. It was intended mainly for use in rural areas. In all, it was meant to move a payload of 15 tons, divided between the tractor and trailer. This vehicle, delivered to Portuguese West Africa, was fitted with a 60-HP six-cylinder gasoline engine. The final drive of the rear axle had a differential lock. Special attention was devoted to the cooling. The normal truck radiator was enlarged at the bottom, greatly increasing the supply of cooling water. Also, additional water containers were installed on the left and right sides of the motor. The vehicle itself weighed 5.7 tons. It was contracted for by a Berlin export firm. Only one vehicle was built.

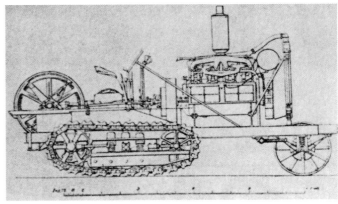

The ancestor of all halftrack vehicles was the "Caterpillar" built by Holt in California around 1890. It was used by various armies as an off-road artillery tractor.

Daimler's Marienfelde works delivered a farm truck with a trailer to Portuguese West Africa in 1908-09.

There the vehicle was equipped with two additional pairs of wheels before and behind the rear axle, so as to decrease ground pressure, because of the poor road conditions there.

When this vehicle was used in Africa, it was soon apparent that the off-road capability of the truck was not always sufficient for the bad roads of the continent. Despite the use of sand tires there were constant problems, which were solved in part by the following means: by adding pairs of wheels before and behind the rear axle, the possibility was created of increasing the ground contact markedly by means of a narrow steel chain. The power for this chain, which was pierced in the middle, came merely from friction. The added pairs of wheels were merely road and steering wheels. The chain was tightened by varying the distance of the forward additional axle to the vehicle's frame. With this solution, initial experience with halftrack vehicles was gained.

In this way a halftrack vehicle, which proved itself within its possibilities, was created for the first time.

After these first, hesitant attempts, years passed before this drive principle was taken up again.

The first months of World War I inspired the wish for a certain independence of motor vehicles from the existing, sometimes very poor network of roads. Thus, the suggestions of Engineer Hugo G. Bremer, who wanted to build an "overland wagon," fell on fertile ground. Since Bremer declined any cooperation with the Traffic Technical Testing Commission (VPK), the War Ministry (KM) put the Inspection of Motor Vehicles (Ikraft) in charge of further dealings. The contract finally signed by Bremer and the War Ministry (A 7 V) on July 19, 1915, required, among others, the following performance:

Two to three tons of load, half lashed down and half not, were to be carried on country roads or across fields in hilly country for 80 kilometers in twelve hours. This was to be done with a normal four-ton truck fitted with the running gear of the Bremer system.

The tests were to be completed by the end of September 1915 at the latest. The Daimler works in Berlin-Marienfelde provided two chassis of the "ALZ 13 b" truck type for the tests.

The first attempts by Engineer Bremer to create an off-road vehicle came to grief because of the technical failings of the time. The picture shows the prototype of the first "Bremerwagen."

In 1916, 20 test vehicles of the "Bremer" model were ordered and became the basis of the state-supported "A.L.Z. 13" truck made by Daimler.

The second test vehicle of the "Bremerwagen" added front and rear tracked running gear to the "A.L.Z. 13." The payload of the test version in 1916 was 2.5 tons.

In 1916 production of the "Bremerwagen" was moved to Marienfelde, and from then on the vehicle was called the "Marienwagen."

After tedious negotiations between the military agencies and Engineer Bremer, a model vehicle could finally be displayed in Neheim on October 6, 1916. Twenty "Bremer-Wagen" were then ordered. The issuing of further contracts appeared to depend on experience gained with the use of these vehicles.

It would be an error to believe that one had found an off-road-capable vehicle in the "Bremer-Wagen." Of the two pairs of tracks that were installed in place of wheels, only the rear pair were driven. Insufficient steering ability and inadequate stability of the tracks showed the system's failings. Of the twenty vehicles under construction, only fifteen were finished.

This production was carried out from 1916 on at the Marienfelde works, where the vehicle was developed further, with extensive improvements, into the "Marienwagen I." Front wheels were still replaced by the still-undriven front tracks, which were as little satisfactory as those of the "Bremer-Wagen." Finally a normal front axle with wheels and tires was installed again.

On November 8, 1916, the War Ministry reported to the OHL that the construction of off-road vehicles had been attempted by various agencies without success. The suggestion of possibly armoring the vehicles was opposed because their carrying capacity was too meager. Yet ten such vehicles were contracted for, and were to be delivered by the spring of 1917.

In 1918 the "Marienwagen I" was fitted experimentally with armor. Only a prototype was built. The upper picture shows the vehicle with the wooden prototype body.

Since the version with front tracks was in no way satisfactory, the normal front axle was eventually reinstalled. This picture shows the "Marienwagen" version with a normal front axle.

On November 11, 1916, the OHL asked the War Ministry to determine whether the specified armored trucks (overland vehicles) could be ready for delivery by spring. Although on January 23, 1917, the establishment of "Assault Armored Vehicle Units" 1 and 2 was announced by A 2 of the War Ministry, and it was determined that the (Bremer) Overland Armored Vehicles would be assigned by the Ikraft, this order was rescinded on April 2, 1917, since the OHL had to declare in mid-March 1917 that the "Bremer-Wagen" were unsuitable for their purposes.

According to an overview of January 30, 1917, the following armored halftrack vehicles of the Bremer type were under contract: ten 45 HP four-ton normal Daimler chassis with track drive. The armor was to be 9 mm thick. They carried as weapons: two machine guns, two Plz-K (Becker), flamethrowers, and close-combat weapons. One of these vehicles was actually finished.

The fifteen "Bremer-Wagen" finished as of then, plus ten "Marienwagen I," were converted into conventional trucks. On order of the War Ministry (A 4), Ikraft was empowered to promote the design of a wheeled-tracked vehicle. This was viewed primarily as an anti-tank vehicle. The Lanz firm was assigned the contract for it. In its final design, though, the firm presented a fully tracked vehicle.

The next step in developing the "Marienwagen" was the replacement of the previous rear track drive with a Holt design, such as was also used in the "A 7 V" tank. The resulting "Marienwagen II" was intended to be a platform vehicle for anti-aircraft and anti-tank guns. Since the steering by normal front wheels was still unsatisfactory, a pair of tracks was again installed. A balance of the load from the rear to the non-driven front tracks was planned. The work on it could not be finished until autumn 1918.

On December 13, 1917, the OHL decided that the "Orionwagen" was also not to be armored. Meanwhile, all other test models of off-road vehicles still on hand were likewise to be eliminated for use as fighting vehicles.

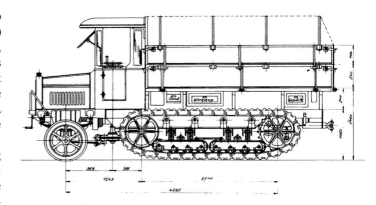

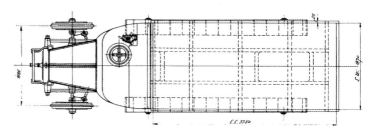

The difficulties with the tracks of the "Marienwagen I" could not be eliminated; thus, as of 1918 an improved track drive to a Holt design was used, and the vehicle was designated "Marienwagen II." The drawing shows the main dimensions of the vehicle.

Series production of the *Marienwagen* II began at the Marienfelde works of the Daimler firm (photographed in autumn 1918).

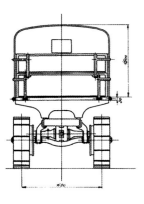

The "Marienwagen II" performs off-road. 44 of them had been produced.

A good view of the "Marienwagen II."

In spite of that, a "motor vehicle procurement program" established by the OHL on October 23, 1918, on the basis of a discussion with the Chefkraft determined, among other things, that the new "Marienwagen II," as well as the Lanz "Raupenwagen," were to be fitted with guns and light armor.

170 of the "Marienwagen II" were ordered, and 44 were built. One tracked-vehicle column with eight vehicles actually reached the front in October 1918. The mounting of anti-tank guns on the vehicles produced later continued in November 1918.

The fact that, on the basis of a suggestion by the APK on October 7, 1918, a varicolored paint job was ordered for armored vehicles, is interesting. As of July 1918, this paint scheme was required for all military equipment.

On account of the war situation, all experiments in the building of off-road vehicles had to be limited to the normal chassis of Army Truck 13, and thus of 4-to-5-ton trucks. Motors of 35 to 50 HP were installed in these chassis. To be sure, the War Ministry ordered on February 10, 1917, that the Marienwagen be fitted with motors of about 100 HP, with the payload accordingly increased to 4 to 5 tons, as opposed to the original 2.5 tons of the Bremer-Wagen.

After the first British tanks appeared, the building of guns suitable for anti-tank defense and mounted on the "Marienwagen II" was foreseen.

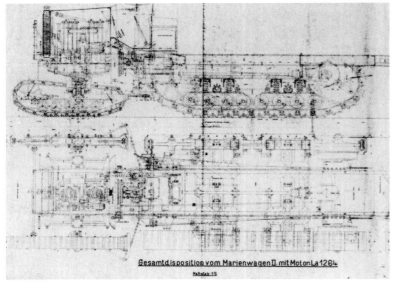

Gesamtdisposition vom Marienwagen II. mit Motor La 1264.
Maßstab 1:5

Since the front wheels could only be steered slightly in rough terrain, the "Marienwagen II" was also fitted with front tracks again. The drawing shows the technical layout of the chassis.

The "Marienwagen II" with front tracks was a solution that was also unsatisfactory.

The "Marienwagen II" was also less than fully satisfactory. Thus, Daimler created the design for the "Marienwagen III," which was laid out as a fully tracked vehicle, with the front axle eliminated.

Simultaneously with the Daimler firm's experiments with the "Marienwagen," the Benz works in Gaggenau was carrying out similar developmental work. Using a normal "3 K 2" truck, they replaced the rear axle with a simple tracked running gear. A second test version was given the rear axle of the "KP" limber, with tracks and road wheels. During the tests, among other things, the front axles were fitted with non-powered tracks. Similarly to the Bremer-Wagen, though, this arrangement seriously weakened the steering. The tracks also came off frequently. The third and final version had a track design that resembled that of the limber, having springs to tighten the tracks, but without normal road wheels. According to existing information, some 25 such vehicles (five of the first type, twenty of the third) were delivered to the army.

In the summer of 1917, a towing vehicle for light artillery—the so-called "Kraftprotze" (power limber)—was created. The first test version had simple tracks with the noses of the chains reaching into the iron tires of the large rear wheels. The front and small rear leading wheels ran on stiff axles that were braced against the rear axle. This forerunner of the power limber already showed considerable advantages in terms of ground adhesion, and thus in towing performance. Further test vehicles had leading wheels suspended on quarter-elliptic springs, and the length of the tracks was also increased. At the front of the vehicle an extender with a support wheel was attached, so that wide ditches could be spanned.

The Benz firm also sought a solution to this problem, and equipped several Type "3 K 2" trucks with rear tracks. Here is a vehicle (1917) of the second type, with the tracks of the "KP" limber.

The Benz-Braeuer "Kraftprotze" limber was begun in 1917 as an artillery tractor, and originally appeared as a wheeled vehicle, which could be changed into a halftrack by adding more road wheels. The pictures show the first test version.

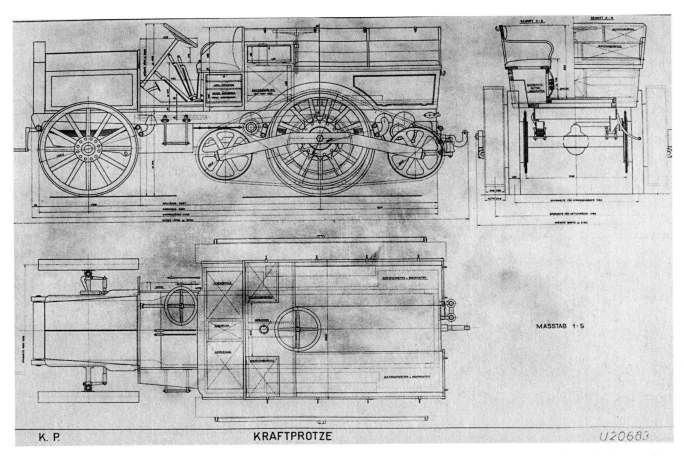

K. P.   KRAFTPROTZE   U20683

The final version of the "KP" vehicle proposed a changeable drive controllable from the freight space. The drawing shows the layout of the vehicle.

A test model of the "Kraftprotze" is seen in rough terrain. The picture shows that the running gear could handle uneven terrain.

Fifty of this vehicle were finished by the war's end. They did not see service and had to be scrapped.

Since all these vehicles had only limited use because of their low top speed, and did not have the needed off-road towing power, a new design was called for. Fifty of the final version of the "Kraftprotze" had been made when the war ended in 1918, but they were never put into service and had to be scrapped. Two hundred had originally been ordered. The vehicle itself came in two versions: the Benz-Braeuer artillery tractor, and the combined gun and troop transporter. Using an eccentric controlled by a handwheel, the track drive could be raised or lowered, so as to use either the wheels or the tracks to drive the vehicle. This shifting simultaneously made the gear ratio of the track drive twice as great as the wheel drive. The chassis was also intended for a fast combat vehicle, but it was never built.

There was no field use of armored halftrack vehicles during World War I.

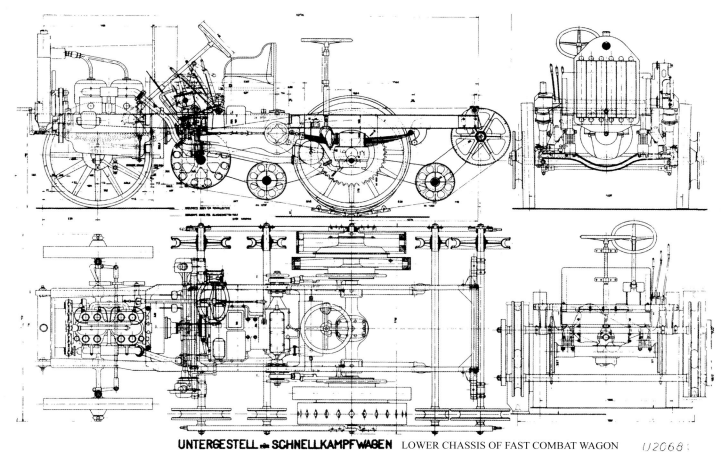

UNTERGESTELL des SCHNELLKAMPFWAGEN   LOWER CHASSIS OF FAST COMBAT WAGON   *U2068*

There were many attempts to use this vehicle in armored form as a fast combat wagon. This development, which was not carried out, bore the type designation "SK." The front track mounting was no longer stiff, but could be swung around the axle of the large track wheel. Thus, the front track drive could be pressed onto the ground, so that the front wheels rose from the surface.

Right after the war ended the police, for their use of armored vehicles on streets for police purposes, tested an armored vehicle on the "Marienwagen II" chassis. The project did not go beyond this testing.

B. Unarmored Halftrack Vehicles, 1919-1945

The question of obtaining towing tractors for the *Reichswehr* in the early postwar years was seen critically, even though the materials for making them were never available in sufficient quantities. A Defense Department memo of April 17, 1928, called for replacing the earlier Krupp-Daimler wheeled towing vehicles with modern tractors. To increase off-road speeds, tracked running gear units were attached experimentally to available chassis, or variable track/wheel drives were tried. The J. A. Maffei AG of Munich-Allach was chiefly interested in this development, and originally equipped their stock "ZW 10" wheel tractor with a lowerable rear track unit.

The model of the Orion-Wagen (April 1917).

Right after the war's end, the police tested an armored "Marienwagen II," but the tests had to be abandoned because of the Treaty of Versailles.

The Duerkopp firm of Bielefeld began work in 1926 on the design of a halftrack vehicle meant to carry the 7.7 cm or 8.8 cm Flak gun.

Chain-tightening wheels and road wheels were attached firmly to the chassis. The rear drive wheels were united with the other parts of the running gear by attaching tracks, forming a halftrack system. Changing from wheel to track drive could be done in a very short time. In 1930, the improved "MSZ 201" version appeared; 24 of them were delivered to the *Reichswehr* as tracked vehicles. A four-cylinder, 60-HP Magirus gasoline engine was installed. A ten-man crew or a payload of 1000 kg could be carried. The vehicle weighed 5.4 tons; the towed load limit was six tons. The "MSZ 10" differed from the customary road towing machine in that attaching tracks also allowed off-road use. Through the special layout of the running gear it was possible to transfer part of the front-axle load to the rear tracks, which essentially ruled out lowering the front wheels and made the steering easier, but also increased the adhesion of tracks and ground.

A skid attached between the radiator bracket and front axle prevented drive components mounted low in the frame from getting stuck in the ground. A similar purpose was served by the side spare wheels, which served as support rollers.

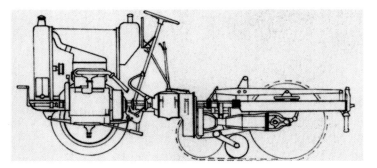

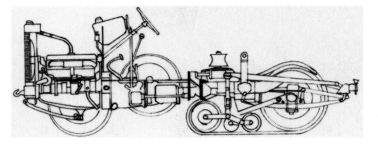

The drawings at upper right offer a comparison of the "ZW 10" and "MSZ 201" vehicles, the latter vehicle being developed especially for military use.

The "MSSZ 201" served as a road vehicle with its tracks removed and its auxiliary running gear raised. The spare wheels were used as movable support rollers. The *Reichswehr* ordered 24 of these vehicles.

As a "tracked machine" with its tracks in place and divided load, it also served as an off-road artillery towing tractor. A 60-HP Magirus gasoline engine powered the vehicle.

In order to secure the longitudinal relation of the rear axle to the middle of the vehicle when driving on tracks, the rear axle was attached to the frame by a direct connection, so that the axle's freedom of movement was not otherwise influenced.

The fast gear installed behind the normal gearbox allowed speeds up to 50 kph on the road, and let the needed high off-road pulling power to be attained in direct drive.

To pull larger loads the vehicle was equipped with a winch, the towing power of which was at most 3000 kg. The winch was powered by an Auxiliary drive on the left side of the gearbox. The winch cable was about 100 meters long.

A built-in air pump was used to inflate the tires easily. At the end of the vehicle was a movable trailer hitch.

According to the test results as of January 1, 1930, the development of these tractors, which were described as stock wheel tractors improved for military use and fitted with auxiliary track drive for off-road use, was nearly completed. As towing machines for light and medium artillery and army engineer uses, there was also a development of the Duerkopp works available, while the Maffei tractor, as already noted, was in production. A towing tractor for heavy artillery was temporarily postponed, and a similar decision was made as to a light towing tractor for heavy infantry guns.

The principle of basing army motorization on central and western European road conditions basically determined the designs of new towing tractors to be developed. A network of paved roads required more than average road speeds, as well as sufficient off-road towing power. Halftrack vehicles appeared to meet these requirements best.

But the task of developing a tracked vehicle for high speeds appeared to be an almost hopeless undertaking at that time. Despite intensive testing activity, especially in Britain, speeds around 20 kph were not always in the realm of technical possibility in 1926.

The renowned "Kegresse" halftrack running gear, which was used widely.

The life span of the tracks averaged about 2000 kilometers. Even the French Kegresse halftrack vehicles reached speeds of only 25 kph, and their tracks lasted 3000 to 5000 kilometers.

Thus, WaPruef 6 was compelled to proceed deliberately from the fully tracked vehicle in developing German halftrack vehicles. After initial tests with rubber tracks instead of chains, it soon became clear that only steel tracks could meet the requirements in terms of stability and life span, as well as the replacement of damaged parts. Thus, the endurance of tracked running gear at high speeds had to be lowered considerably, the life span had to be increased, and the noise had to be decreased. Through systematic testing work, a tracked running gear could be developed that would essentially equal the established requirements. Especially valuable in this respect was an established test center for running gear of tracked vehicles that allowed speeds up to 80 kph and vehicle weights up to 20 tons. Thus, the following criteria were considered:

- the total resistance of a given tracked running gear depending on speed, performance, vehicle weight, and slippage.
- Rolling resistance and bearing friction of the road wheels depending on speed and vehicle weight.

- Free-wheeling resistance of the tracks after removal of the road wheels.

From the test results there emerged a tracked running gear with the following special features:

- lubricated track links
- large road wheels
- front drive of the tracks
- toothed gears on the drive wheels
- rubber tires for road, leading, and driving wheels
- rubber pads to protect the track links

By the use of such features, speeds of up to 50 kph on paved roads gave the following results:

- the resistance was only 5 to 10% higher than that of wheeled vehicles
- the resistance to wear came very close to that of ordinary wheels and tires
- the noise level was not higher than that of older trucks with chain-driven rear wheels.

Thus, this running gear guaranteed high speeds from comparatively low power. Only the sensitivity of the steering for road travel could not be attained with the known steering apparatus. To dispose of this problem, the vehicles were also equipped with front wheels that, in and of themselves, allowed only the handling of mild curves and direction correction at high speeds, while sharp curves were taken by influencing the steering gear with normal steering. The use of lubricated steel track links also allowed the desired towing power through the correct extent of the tracks. A design of the entire vehicle that departed from any connection with stock truck design had allowed the creation of a type of towing vehicle that became highly superior to all known types, by taking certain faults in the bargain.

Ernst Kniepkamp was responsible for the technical design of these vehicles. He had worked at the Army Weapons Office since 1925, and become the civilian chief of the WaPruef 6 department in 1936.

After determining needs and choosing models, the development of the vehicles was turned over to contracted firms that essentially carried out the systematic development and testing of the prototypes, and prepared the vehicles for series production.

The building program foreseen at that time included the following towing vehicles:

A comparison of the six basic types of towing vehicles used by the German *Wehrmacht*. The drawings on the facing page are illustrated by the photo. From left to right: 1-ton, 3-ton, 5-ton, 8-ton, 12-ton, and 18-ton towing vehicles.

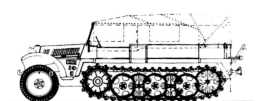

Light 1-ton towing vehicle (Sd.Kfz. 10) DEMAG Type "D 7"

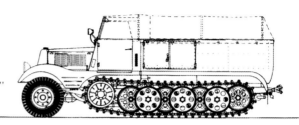

Light 3-ton towing vehicle (Sd.Kfz. 11) HANOMAG Type "H kl 6"

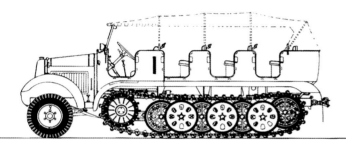

Light 5-ton towing vehicle (Sd.Kfz. 6) Buessing-NAG Type "BN 9"

Medium 8-ton towing vehicle (Sd.Kfz. 7) Krauss-Maffei Type "KM m 11"

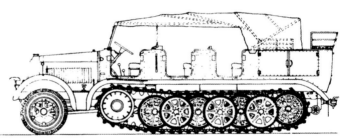

Heavy 12-ton towing vehicle (Sd.Kfz. 8) Daimler-Benz Type "DB 10"

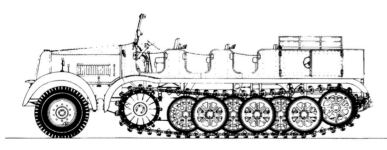

Heavy 18-ton towing vehicle (Sd.Kfz. 9) FAMO Type "F 3"

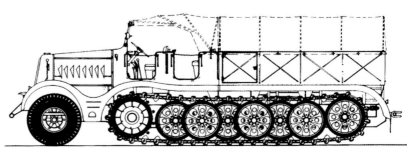

1-ton halftrack series	Maker: Demag AG, Wetter/Ruhr
3-ton halftrack series	Maker: Hansa-Lloyd-Goliath AG
5-ton halftrack series	Maker: Buessing-NAG, Berlin-Oberschoenewiede
8-ton halftrack series	Maker: Krauss-Maffei AG, Munich-Allach
12-t0n halftrack series	Maker: Daimler-Benz AG, Berlin-Marienfelde
18-ton halftrack series	Maker: Famo, Breslau

After the development of the vehicles was finished, so-called subsidiary building firms were included, which took part in the production.

The technical design of the vehicles basically followed the same guidelines. These halftrack vehicles with rubber-tired front axles and rear tracks were driven by a six- or twelve-cylinder Maybach motor, which activated a gearbox through a plate clutch, the gearbox including change, reduction, and steering gears in a single multipart housing. The steering gear took on the double job of equalizing and steering gears. Via stiff-coupled side shafts and spur-gear transmission, the front-mounted track drive wheels were powered. The nonpowered front axle was almost always connected to the frame by leaf springs, while the track running gear had half-elliptic springs at first, while later versions were usually fitted with torsion bars. The frame almost always consisted of two welded longitudinal members with welded-in U- and transverse tube members.

1-ton Halftrack Series and Light *Wehrmacht* Tractor

In 1934, the question of producing the necessary towing vehicle still required thorough testing. The release of these towing vehicles for series production was to take place as of September 1, 1934. If

necessary, a three-axle truck was planned as a temporary solution. Preparatory work on this light vehicle at the Wetter/Ruhr works of the Demag AG created prototypes that were tested thoroughly in 1934-35. They were Types "D 11 1" and "D 11 2," both of which were fitted with the BMW 6-cylinder, 28-HP Type "315" motor. The third prototype ("D 11 3") was fitted with the more powerful Type "319" motor in 1936. Some of these vehicles had fully rubber-tired (shot-secure) front axles. In 1936-37 the Type "D 4" appeared as a project, but this vehicle was not built, and existed only in the form of plans. It was intended to have the Maybach four-cylinder, 65-HP "HL 25" gasoline engine. The calculated overall weight was 3750 kg, and the trailer load was 600 kg. The track width of the tracks was 1500 mm. With external dimensions of 4750 x 1900 x 1750 mm, the basic structure was the same as the Type "D 11 3." The successor Type "D 6," built from 1937 to 1938, went into production with a Maybach "HL 38" motor in its temporary final form, and was planned as the standard towing vehicle for the 3.7 cm Pak, the Special Trailer 32, the 2 cm Flak, and the Light Infantry Gun 18.

In part, these prototypes were also equipped with shot-secure front tires. The upper left picture shows the third prototype towing the 3.7 cm Pak.

The third prototype had different running gear. The distance between the front wheels and drive wheels was also increased (upper right).

Left column, from top to bottom: the Demag AG developed the Type "D 11 1" for towing light loads. It is shown here with a rear-mounted BMW "315" motor.

The first vehicle was followed in 1935 by the second prototype "D 11 2," which was still not accepted for production. Only the driving-technical requirements could be fulfilled by it.

The third prototype "D 11 3" was fitted with the more powerful BMW "319" motor in 1936. Increased troop capacity was now considered.

The top view shows the layout of the driver's seat and those of the crew.

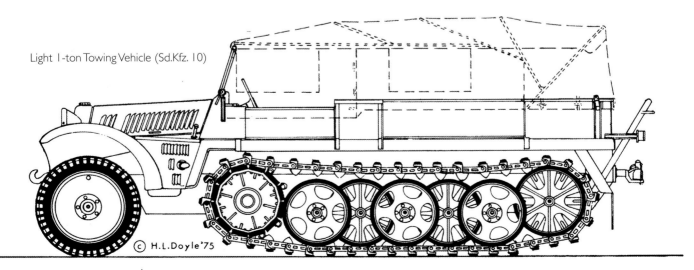

Light 1-ton Towing Vehicle (Sd.Kfz. 10)

© H.L.Doyle '75

The pre-production and production model "D 6" or "D 7" at left was built in this firm until 1944. It served to tow the 3.7 cm Pak, the light Infantry Gun 18, the 2 cm Flak 30, and the Ammunition Trailer 32.

The left central picture shows the driver's compartment of the one-ton towing vehicle. To the driver's right is the semi-automatic "Variorex" gearbox.

The tracks of the one-ton vehicle include the drive wheel, the alternating road wheels, and the leading wheel at the rear (right center).

During the war, nearly 17,500 of the 1-ton towing vehicle were built to tow antitank guns, and were used for many other supplying tasks (below, left, and right).

The final version ("D 7"), built from 1938 to 1944, originally still had the "NL 38" motor, and later the 100 HP "HL 42" motor as its powerplant. This vehicle was officially called "Light Towing Vehicle 1-ton" (Sd. Kfz. 10). The vehicle was built not only by Demag, but also by Adler, Buessing-NAG, Mechanische Werke Cottbus, MIAG, M.N.H.-Hannover, and the Saurer works in Vienna. On December 20, 1942, there were 11,116 of these vehicles with various units of the *Wehrmacht*. In 1943 2724 of these vehicles were built, while in 1944 the year's production numbered 873 units. In all, some 17,500 of the one-ton towing vehicle were built.

In January 1943, Hitler had already mentioned that the one-ton towing vehicle should be phased out in favor of increased production of the three-ton type. During the war well-known French firms, including Peugeot, Renault, Lorraine, Panhard, and Simca, were also called into this building program.

The Gaubschat firm of Berlin prepared vehicles of the one-ton series for the large Telephone Troop a (mot.). The vehicle ran as Special Vehicle 10/1 as a gas detector truck for the fog troops. It served to carry crews and equipment to find traces of poison gas. Eight-men crews were planned. The fog troops also used the Sd. Kfz. 10/2, the light detoxification vehicle. It was used to lay coverings of detoxifying material on areas in the country that had been covered with poison gas. Loaded trailers could also be towed. Four-man crews were planned. The third vehicle (Sd. Kfz. 10/3) saw service as the light spraying vehicle. With this vehicle, off-road areas up to 16 meters wide could be sprayed with immobile materials. A container installed on the back, with a capacity of 500 liters, was put under pressure by an air compressor. Another vehicle of this series was used as a self-propelled mount for the 2 cm Flak 30 gun. On the vehicle itself were carried: the weapon, which could be turned 360 degrees; the full crew of seven men; small parts of gun equip-

The first variation was the externally almost unchanged "Gasspuerer-Kraftwagen" (Sd. Kfz. 10/1). With an eight-man crew, the weight of the built-in equipment was 150 kg.

The "leichte Entgiftungs-Kraftwagen" (Sd. Kfz. 10/2) followed. The crew consisted of four men, and the detoxifying substance load was 400 kg. The holding capacity of the spreading box was 200 kg, and a spreading distance of one meter was attained.

The last vehicle for the "fog troops" was the "leichte Spruehkraftwagen" 9Sd. Kfz. 10/3), which was suited for laying off-road routes. The contents of the container was 500 liters. Laying and spreading were done by compressed air by means of a swinging apparatus. Courses up to 16 meters wide could be laid.

The Sd. Kfz. 10/4 was a self-propelled mount for the 2 cm Flak 30 gun. The picture shows one of the early "D II 3" prototypes as a basis for this development.

This picture shows the vehicle before the gun was installed. The sidewalls could be folded down to extend the gun platform.

The vehicle and weapon were originally unprotected, which soon caused heavy losses. Because of its height, the gun was first fitted with an armor shield.

Later, armored cabs were also used, which made the ground action of these vehicles easier.

ment; and 280 rounds of ammunition. The rest of the equipment was carried on a one-axle trailer. The top speed was 50 kph. The designation of this vehicle was "Self-propelled mount with 2 cm Flak 30) (Sd. Kfz. 10/4). Some of them were fitted during the war with armored cabs and protective shields for the guns.

The 3.7 cm and 5 cm antitank guns were also installed in a makeshift manner. With minor changes (omitting one pair of road wheels), the chassis also became the basis for the light armored vehicle (Sd. Kfz. 250).

Last in the series was the Project "D 8," which appeared in 1939. This vehicle, though, only existed in drawings. The Maybach "HL 42" motor was also planned for it, but the overall weight was increased to 5800 kg. The top speed was to be 74 kph, and the outside dimensions were to be 7070 x 1824 x 1750 mm.

The Adler Werke AG of Frankfurt am Main had received a contract in 1937 to create a similar series of light halftrack towing vehicles. The development took place under the designation "HK. 300." The first vehicles of this series, with the type designation "A

During the war, these vehicles were used as self-propelled mounts for 3.7 and 5 cm antitank guns.

The HK. 300 series developed by the Adler works was to replace the existing one-ton towing vehicle series. The pictures show side and front views of the first prototype of this series, Type "A 1." The series did not go beyond prototypes.

1," were built in 1938-39 and equipped with the four-cylinder, 65 HP Maybach "HL 25" gasoline engine. In their general structure, they very much resembled the Demag series. In 1939 the second prototype, "A 2," appeared, using the more powerful 78 HP Maybach "HL 28" motor and having a gross weight of 2600 kg. The third prototype, "A 3," built in 1939-40, also used the Maybach "HL 25" engine, and weighed 3450 kg. A variant of this vehicle was the Type "A 3 F" which, equipped with the "HL 28" motor, was planned as a closed staff car. The final version of the series appeared in 1941, and a test model of this "Light Towing Machine HK. 301" was delivered on 16 August 1941, with four more following. A contract for the building of a zero series of 50 vehicles was assigned, but the vehicles themselves were never built.

Hitler's call for very simplified towing vehicles in 1941 led to a request by the Army Weapons Office to Adler on 7 May 1942 to create a towing vehicle with a trailer load of three tons. The projected beginning of production was to be the spring of 1943. The first two prototypes of the so-called "Light *Wehrmacht* Tractor" were built in 1942 and 1943, and equipped with the four-cylinder, 95 HP Maybach

The pictures from top to bottom show the second prototype, which followed in 1939, with the designation "A 2."

The A 2 vehicle was also tried with various bodies.

Early in 1940 the "A 3" prototype was available. It is seen here with a troop-carrier body.

The prototype "A 3 F" with a closed body was conceived as a staff vehicle.

The final vehicle of the "HK 300" series was the "HK 301," which likewise did not go into series production.

Starting in 1942, Adler developed prototypes of a "Light *Wehrmacht* Tractor," of which only three versions became known. This picture shows the first prototype, with armor for the driver's compartment and motor.

The second prototype shows similar bodywork. Here, too, there was no series production. The vehicles were to be used as supply trucks, towing tractors, and self-propelled gun mounts.

"HL 30" motor. These vehicles, sometimes armored, were also to serve as self-propelled mounts. In 1944 came the third prototype, now equipped with the Maybach "HL 42" engine. The total weight was 8210 kg. A ZF-Adler four-speed gearbox with auxiliary drive was chosen for installation, and the disc brakes already used in the "*Raupenschlepper Ost*" were also installed. Ungreased tracks formed a typical identifying mark of this series. The war's events no longer allowed the production of these vehicles, and only these prototypes were built. The development ended in 1944 with the Halftrack Vehicle 305, which was planned as a project and was built just like the third prototype of the Light *Wehrmacht* Tractor, with a Maybach-"OLVAR" gearbox intended.

Because of the shortage of towing vehicles, Speer made a suggestion in October 1944 that a "low towing vehicle" be built. Hitler expressed the opinion on 1 November 1944 "that for this the components of the one-ton tractor were especially suited, while the

gearbox and other power-train aggregates could be taken over from the three-ton towing vehicle."

Three-ton Halftrack and HK. 600 Series

This development, conducted by the Hansa-Lloyd-Goliath AG of Bremen, began in 1933 and created its first prototype, the "HL.kl.2" vehicle. Equipped with a six-cylinder "Type 3500" engine, the complete vehicle weighed some five tons and had a listed pulling power of three tons. The improved "HL.kl.3" version appeared in 1935 and already had the dummy radiator of all the following models.

At this time, tests were already begun on making these vehicles suitable for armored bodies by installing the motor at the rear. The vehicles that resulted from these tests were designated "HL.kl.3" (H) and, as of 1936, "HL.kl.4 (H)." The end of this development in 1938 resulted in the Type "H 8 (H)," for which the Hanomag firm was responsible.

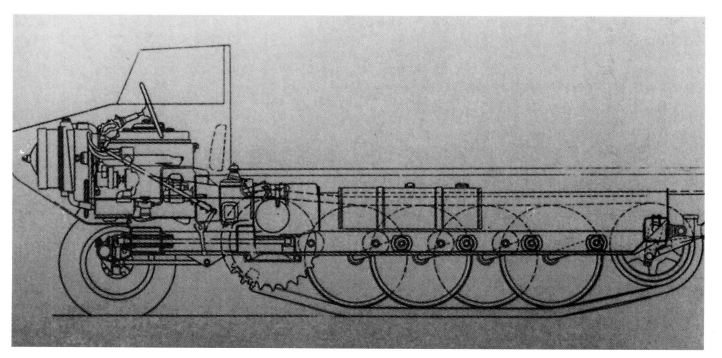

Only drawings of the third prototype exist. They show the torsion-bar arrangement of the running gear.

In 1936 there already appeared the production version of the vehicle, the Type "HL.kl.5" (chassis numbers 1937 320 001-320 195, 1938 320 196-320 506), which was still fitted with the 3.5-litrer Hansa-Lloyd motor. With a weight of 6.5 tons, the vehicle was used for towing the light field howitzer (10.5 cm le F.H. 18), an ammunition trailer, or for the medium minelayer. The price of the vehicle (without a cable winch) was 20,000 Reichsmark. The official designation of the vehicle was "Light Towing Wagon 3t (Sd. Kfz. 11)."

The "HL.kl.2" chassis shows the typical construction of German halftrack vehicles.

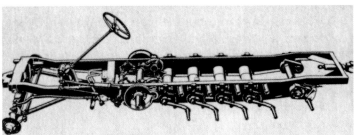

One of the first prototypes of the three-ton halftrack and HK.600 series was the Type "HL.kl.2" built by Hansa-Lloyd-Goliath in 1934 (above left).

The frame of the "HL.kl.2" with swinging arms for the tracked running gear (left).

The Type "HL.kl.3," which appeared in 1936, already showed the final form of the radiator grille. Only slight changes from its predecessor had been made.

The picture shows one of the pre-series vehicles towing a 10.5 cm leFH (3-ton light towing wagon, Sd. Kfz. 11).

The "HL kl 5" pre-series vehicle had the final appearance of the production model, but it showed several differences in its running gear. The inner road wheels were still made as full wheels.

These pictures (above and following) show the last version of this series as a chassis and its performance in rough country (Type H kl 6).

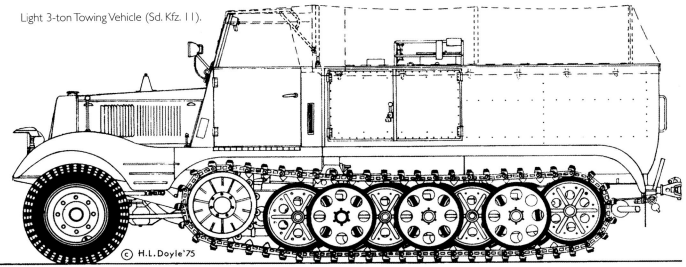

Light 3-ton Towing Vehicle (Sd. Kfz. 11).

© H.L. Doyle '75

Left and right side views of the production form of the 3-ton medium towing vehicle (Sd. Kfz. 11). The ammunition was stored in side compartments, and the gun crew entered from the rear.

A few three-ton vehicles were also fitted with customary engineer bodies with side entry.

Four chassis types were originally included in the planning: Types "H kl 6" (Sd.Kfz. 11), "H kl 6 n" (Sd.Kfz. 11/1), "H kl 6 s" (Sd.Kfz. 11/2), and "H kl 6 k" (Sd.Kfz. 11/3). Every chassis type was different in details of its frame design. The type designations also indicated that Hanomag of Hannover had taken over the further development of these vehicles. As of 1938, Hanomag also created the final type of "H kl 6," the first series of which were still powered by the Maybach "HL 38 TUKR" motor. Later series were fitted with the Maybach "HL 42 TUKRM" motor, which was built not only by Maybach, but also by the Nordbau GmbH of Berlin-Niederschoe-newiede and the Auto-Union Horch works in Zwickau/Sa. While at first only the firms of Hanomag, Dept. Tb in Hannover-Linden and C. F. W. Borgward (formerly Hansa-Lloyd and Goliath Works in Bremen) produced the chassis (numbers 1939 320507-320830 with HL 38 motor), later the Adlerwerke AG of Frankfurt am Main, directed by Heinrich Kleyer, the Auto-Union Horck Works in Zwickau and the Skodawerke AG, Dept. D-J joined in. The vehicles differed only in the makers' emblems on the radiator grilles.

The tracks, the manufacture of which always resulted in shortages, were made by the Karl Ritscher GmbH, Moorburger Trecker-Werke in Moorburg near Hamburg-Siemag, Siegener Maschinenbau GmbH in Dahlbruch/Westfalen-Adlerwerke AG represented by Heinrich Kleyer in Frankfurt am Main, and the Metallwerke Karl Michler GmbH, Bearbeitungswerk Dept. in Leipzig.

The bodies for these vehicles, which unlike the larger types had longitudinal seat benches for the crews with rear entrances, were made mainly by the firms of Drettmann in Lesum and Bauer in Cologne. A few of the usual engineer bodies were fitted with side entrances, plus the ambulance bodies for the German Sea Rescue Organization.

The firm of C. F. W. Borgward delivered the Auxiliary Drive I for the "H kl 6 s" chassis type, while the "H kl 6 k" chassis type could be had with or without Auxiliary Drive II. Chassis 79512 to 795267 made by Hanomag had a modified fuel tank. The Knorr-Bremse AG firm of Berlin supplied an air compressor for the "H kl 6 k" chassis type.

Until chassis no. 795090 (Hanomag) and 320417 (Hansa-Lloyd) 7.25-20 spare tires were used, while from chassis no. 695091 (Hanomag) and 320418 (Hansa-Lloyd) on, the 190-18 size was used. As of chassis no. 820760, all the fenders for these vehicles were made only by the Auto-Union Horch Works in Zwickau.

The Ford Works in Cologne produced fifteen of these models for testing in 1942.

In September 1942, Hitler was shown the Programm 2 production schedule for towing tractors. Here there was an obvious shift to the armored versions. The "*Raupenschlepper Ost*" was to replace the unarmored one- and three-ton towing vehicles extensively. The stated volume of some 500 vehicles was to be applied to the armored versions. The armored troop carriers, according to figures at hand, saved up to 50% of crew losses. On 20 September 1942 Hitler welcomed the suggestion that, to expand capacities for making armored troop carriers, the unarmored one- and three-ton types by replaced by Opel three-ton trucks with added tracks. In May 1943, the production of armored towing vehicles first climbed to 500 vehicles per month.

The last series had normal truck bodies with wooden sides. The vehicle at the rear has the small war headlights used in the last war year.

The foglaying truck (Sd.Kfz. 11/1) served the fog troops for towing foglayers of various calibers. The ammunition compartments on the sides could be fitted for any caliber.

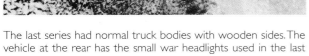

Below: The Medium Detoxifying Wagon (Sd.Kfz. 11/2) here is a brand-new vehicle with body by the Peter Bauer firm.

The last vehicles of the three-ton series were fitted with a wooden rear body and a 16-liter fuel tank. They stayed in production to 1945. On 20 December 1942 4209 of these vehicles were on hand. In 1943 2133 of them were built, and in 1944 another 1308. In all, some 9000 of the three-ton towing vehicle were built.

Other varieties were the foglaying wagon (Sd.Kfz. 11/1) and the medium detoxifying wagon (Sd.Kfz. 11/2). Like the light type, they were also used to produce gases with detoxifying materials in country that had been poisoned with lethal substances. A two-roller spraying device with a capacity of 70 kg was installed. Four men operated the vehicle. Of the medium spraying vehicle, Sd. Kfz. 11/3,

125 were built in 1937 by Drettmann. These vehicles were used by the foglaying troops to lay ground materials. The vehicles had sprayer bodies with tanks, compressed-air systems, and spraying nozzles to spread the materials. Included in this building program were the firms of Knorr-Bremse in Berlin, Konrad Moeller of Berlin, Rudolf Sack of Leipzig, and Weserhütte of Oeynhausen.

The Sd.Kfz. 11/4 and 11/5 were used to tow the 15 cm Foglayer 41 and 21 cm Foglayer 42. The ammunition racks were exchangeable for 10 cm, 15 cm, and 21 cm mortar shells. Along with thirty-six 15 cm or ten 21 cm shells, there was room for a six-man crew including the driver. Also worthy of note is a mechanical hole borer

The detoxifying material—stored in drums in the rear body—was dispensed by a scattering apparatus at the rear of the vehicle.

Some of the three-ton vehicles were fitted with ambulance bodies for the German Sea Rescue Organization. They were used in rescuing shipwreck victims in the dune area.

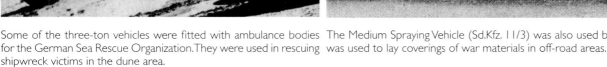

The Medium Spraying Vehicle (Sd.Kfz. 11/3) was also used by the foglaying troops. It was used to lay coverings of war materials in off-road areas.

The Fog Wagon (Sd. Kfz. 11/4) was, like Sd. Kfz. 11/1, used to tow foglayers of various sizes.

on the three-ton vehicle. As per order of 29 January 1936, a mobile searchlight with a 50 cm diameter was also mounted on the same chassis. Presumably only one of them was built.

With minor modifications, the chassis formed the basis of the medium armored vehicle (Sd.Kfz. 251), the medium armored personnel carrier of the German *Wehrmacht*.

In 1943, Hitler advocated the development of a Light Field Howitzer 18/40 with all-around fire on the three-ton towing vehicle, removable onto a cross mount. A similar development was planned for the 7.5 cm Pak 44 (L/70). There were doubts as to the sturdiness of the guns in lateral fire, since the long barrel of the Pak 44 in particular was hard to swing, and lashing it down caused problems. Setting it down from the vehicle was to be decided on only after troop testing, in which a cross mount was not to be used because of the resulting immobility. The removing process, in any case, was to be carried out by using a simple crane carried on the vehicle. In January 1944 the development of the 7.5 cm Pak (L/70) was ordered halted.

Testing of the Light Howitzer 18/40 on the three-ton towing vehicle, on the other hand, was to be carried on quickly. Its use was foreseen as army artillery and in motorized divisions in place of the Light Howitzer 18 mot. Z.

Within the "Fast Program," the Hanomag firm made an attempt in 1939 to create a so-called uniform halftrack vehicle within the three-ton class. Prototypes for it were actually built and designated "H 7." These vehicles, equipped with a Maybach "Variorex" gearbox, looked like the Type "H.kl.6" and were not developed. To replace the three-ton halftrack series, the Hanomag and Demag firms worked since 1939 to develop the HK.600 series. Thus, in 1939-40 there arose the Hanomag Type "HK.601," which looked like the one-ton towing machine. This vehicle was supposed to replace the one- and three-ton towing vehicles. Seven and thirty vehicles were contracted for, and the Demag firm also took part in their production. The vehicles had a gross weight of 6.3 tons and used the Maybach "HL 45 Z" six-cylinder engine. A top speed of 75 kph and a towing capacity of 4.5 tons were expected.

An armored counterpart was designated "HKp 602." The Type "HKp 603" developed by Hanomag was to replace the medium armored troop carrier.

In 1941-42, Demag created the Type "HK. 605," which had an only partly armored, self-bearing frame design. The 170 HP Maybach "HL 50" was to be used as its motor. This vehicle, equipped with Argus disc brakes, had a gross weight of 6.8 tons and a top speed of 71 kph. A somewhat heavier Type "HKp 607" weighing 9.5 tons appeared in 1942 as a Hanomag project. Finally the Demag firm developed the *Schuetzenpanzer* "HKp 606," built as a prototype in 1941-42, to replace all existing armored troop carriers. The seven-ton vehicle was fitted with the Maybach "HL 50" motor, had

In 1939 it was suggested that the Hanomag "H 7" should be the uniform chassis for the three-ton halftrack series.

The Type "HK 601" united features of the one- and three-ton towing machines. Only prototypes were built.

The side and rear views of the "LR 75" vehicle show its layout as a truck.

Outside the German *Wehrmacht's* towing vehicle program, the Daimler-Benz AG introduced a similar vehicle for civilian use in 1937-38. The picture above shows the chassis of this Type "LR 75."

The German *Reichspost* equipped some of these vehicles with bus bodies and used them in high mountain areas.

The Swedish Army also adopted the German tracked running gear. This is the "HBT m/43" artillery tractor built by Volvo.

The five-ton medium towing vehicle (Sd.Kfz. 6) was built by Buessing in 1934-35 as the Type "BN I 5." It used a Maybach "NL 35" motor.

an OL-VAR gearbox and Argus disc brakes. Its measurements were 4850 x 1980 x 1850 mm.

For the sake of completion, we should mention one more half-track, which was not developed by the *Wehrmacht* but followed the usual design tendency. In 1937-38 the Daimler-Benz AG created the Type "LR 75," twenty-five chassis of which were built. Most of them were fitted with bus bodies and used by the *Reichspost* in mountainous areas.

Several three-ton towing vehicles were also sold to other countries during the war. On the basis of the experience thus gained, attempts were made to copy the vehicles. For example, in Sweden the Volvo Type "HBT" (m/43) was built, with its running gear copied directly from the three-ton towing machine.

5-ton Halftrack Series and Heavy *Wehrmacht* Tractor

The start of this development, which was carried out by Buessing-NAG in Berlin-Oberschoeneweide, resulted in the introduction of the "L 4" vehicle in 1934. Fitted with the 85 HP Maybach "NL 35 U" motor, this towing machine was used by artillery units as a "light off-road-capable towing wagon (Sd.Kfz. 6) 1934 Type." Only eight of them (chassis numbers 21501-21508) were built by Buessing-NAG. A copy of the vehicle was made by the Krauss-Maffei AG and designated "KM I 4." In 1935 there appeared the Type "BN I 5" by Buessing-NAG, which was also built by Daimler-Benz as Type

The three-ton light towing vehicle (Sd.Kfz. 11) in its final version.

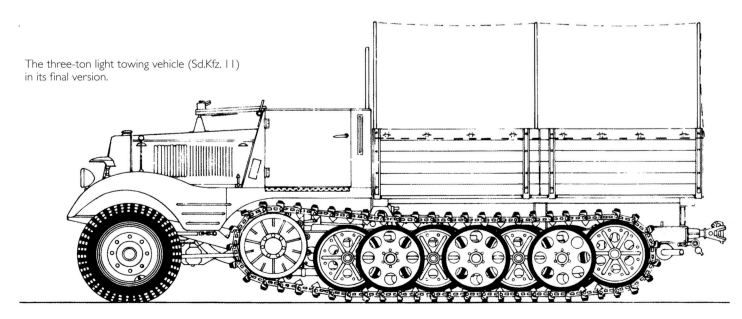

To keep high mountain roads open, a few vehicles of the 5-ton halftrack class were also fitted with snowplows. The body was suited to the new use.

In 1938-39 the Type "BN 18" five-ton towing machine was built, now with lengthened tracks. The picture shows such a vehicle towing a 10.5 cm leFH.

"DB I 5." Still fitted with the "NL 35" motor, the vehicle had a gross weight of 8.8 tons. In 1936 the Type "BN 17" appeared, now with the upgraded six-cylinder Maybach Type "NL 38," which produced 100 HP. Buessing built 280 of them (chassis no. 2201-22481). The vehicle's price was 32,000 Reichsmark. It was intended mainly for towing engineer equipment wagons, but artillery units also used the vehicle for the 10.5 cm le.FH. 18 light howitzer. The bodies

The Type "BN 17" appeared externally unchanged in 1936, now using the Maybach "NL 38" motor. The bodies generally came in two versions. The pictures at left show the vehicle with the engineer body and below with the artillery body.

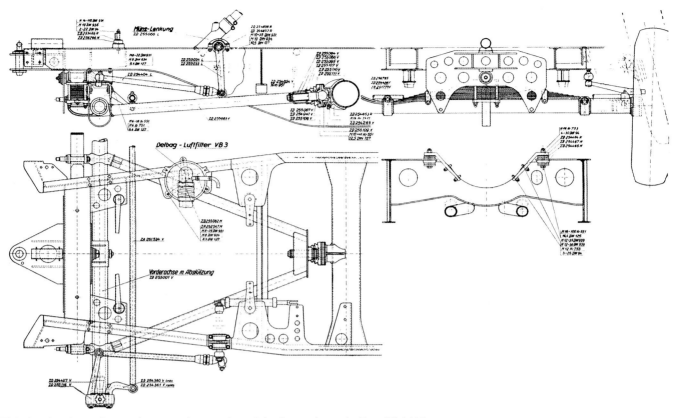

This drawing shows the attachment and suspension of the front axle on the Type "BN 18."

The road wheels of the Type "BN 18" were sprung by torsion bars via crank arms. The drawing also shows the box arrangement of the running gear.

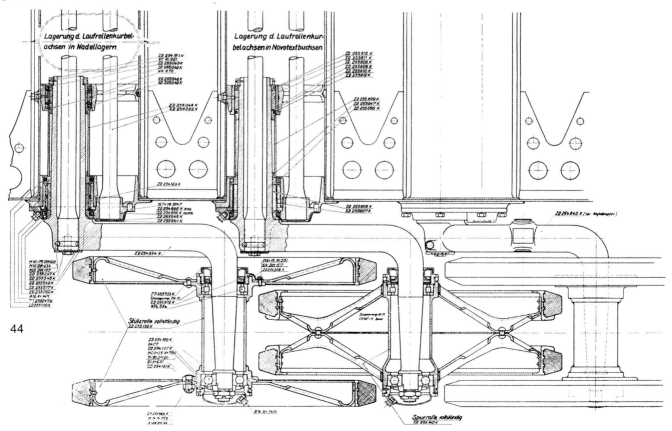

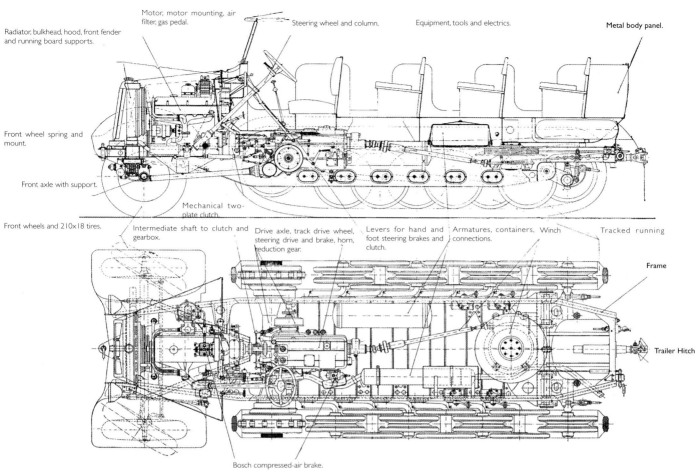

Radiator, bulkhead, hood, front fender and running board supports.

Motor, motor mounting, air filter, gas pedal.

Steering wheel and column.

Equipment, tools and electrics.

Metal body panel.

Front wheel spring and mount.

Front axle with support.

Mechanical two-plate clutch.

Front wheels and 210x18 tires.

Intermediate shaft to clutch and gearbox.

Drive axle, track drive wheel, steering drive and brake, horn, reduction gear.

Levers for hand and foot steering brakes and clutch.

Armatures, containers, connections.

Winch

Tracked running

Frame

Trailer Hitch

Bosch compressed-air brake.

The last version of this series was Type "BN 9" of 1939. The picture shows the vehicle's chassis on display at the International Auto Show in Berlin.

Side views of the chassis and the complete vehicle, with the engineer body.

Rear view of the "BN 9" vehicle with closed body.

differed, and the engineer body provided more seats. The Daimler-Benz version was designated "DB I 7." In 1938 the identical final version, Type "BN I 8" (Daimler-Benz version "DB I 8") followed. The track length was increased from 1270 to 2025 mm, but it still used the Maybach "NL 38" motor. The whole production of this type amounted to 465 units by Buessing, while Daimler-Benz made 272 of them. In 1939 the improved Type "BN 9" was delivered, now using the 115 HP Maybach "HL 45 TURKM" motor. Buessing-NAG delivered 617 of them (chassis no. 3001-3617). A change in the braking system created Type "BN 9 b," production of which ended in November 1943. According to available data, 687 of this vehicle were built by Buessing. It was also made by the Bohemian-Moravian Machine Works in Prague. On 20 December 1942 there were 2061 of these vehicles on hand; in 1943, 563 of them were built, while 1944 production numbered 729 units. In all, some 3500 five-ton towing vehicles were built.

Rear-engined versions of these vehicles for armored bodies were developed starting in 1934, in collaboration with Rheinmetall-Borsig.

Light 5-ton Towing Wagon (Sd.Kfz. 6) with engineer body.

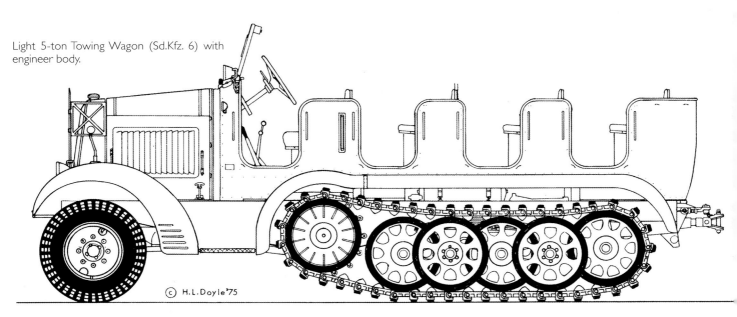

© H.L.Doyle '75

A single example of the "BN 11 V" vehicle (chassis no. 2005) appeared on the Buessing type list. No further data remain. Next came a "BN 10 H" vehicle, three of which (chassis no. 2006-2008) were built. These are obviously rear-engined vehicles. Later two prototypes of the "HKp 901" vehicle (chassis no. 2011 and 2015) were built, leading to the "HKp 902." A variant of this vehicle was designated "HKp 903."

The final version of the five-ton towing vehicle also appeared in two basic forms. The Sd.Kfz. 6/1 with artillery body was used to tow the le.FH. 18, while the Sd.Kfz. 6 was used for Engineer Vehicles PF 10, 11, and 12. The Sd. Kfz. 6/2 was a self-propelled mount for

In action, the side walls were folded up horizontally, leaving the crew essentially unprotected.

As a self-propelled mount (Sd.Kfz. 6/2), the five-ton towing machine carried a 3.7 cm Flak 36.

47

A few examples of partly armored self-propelled mounts using the chassis of the five-ton towing vehicle saw service in North Africa. The vehicles, designated "Diana," carried a Russian 7.62 cm Pak 36 for antitank use.

the 3.7 cm Flak 36. Ammunition for the gun was carried in a single-axle trailer. With a seven-man crew, the vehicle had a total weight of 10.4 tons. It was used chiefly by army anti-aircraft units.

The Army Weapons Office's efforts toward simplification led to the dropping of the five-ton towing wagon in favor of a new design in 1943. The contract for it was assigned by the Army Weapons Office to Buessing-BAG on 7 May 1942, and the first new-type vehicle was to be ready for use in the spring of 1943. A towing vehicle for six-ton trailers and three-ton payloads was called for. The very simplified vehicle had ungreased tracks and used the Maybach "HL 42" motor as its powerplant. This so-called "Heavy *Wehrmacht* Trac-

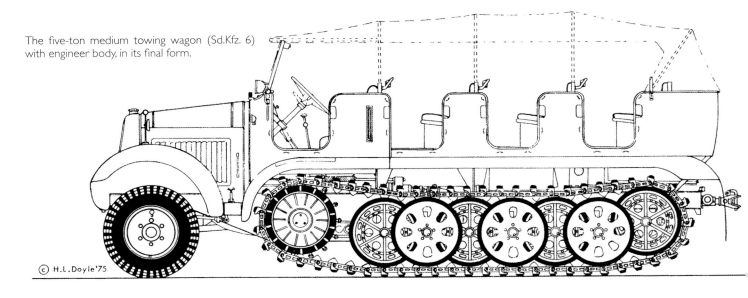

The five-ton medium towing wagon (Sd.Kfz. 6) with engineer body, in its final form.

© H.L. Doyle '75

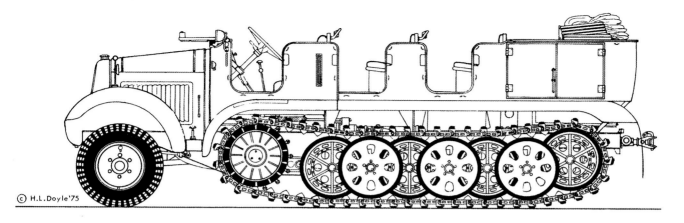

The 5-ton Medium Towing Wagon (Sd.Kfz. 6/1) with artillery body, final version.

The Heavy *Wehrmacht* Tractor (sWS) went into production, and was regarded as a replacement for the five-ton towing wagon. The pictures show front and rear views of the chassis; the ungreased tracks are noticeable.

The Heavy *Wehrmacht* Tractor with a covered rear bed was used as a troop supply truck.

A partly armored version was used to supply the front-line troops.

tor" weighed 13.5 tons and reached a top speed of 29 kph. At first, contracts for the *Wehrmacht* called for 7484 of these vehicles, and the Army Weapons Office tried to increase new production to some 150 vehicles per month by the spring of 1943. Buessing-NAG and Ringhoffer-Tatra in Kolin were the producers. Production actually began with five examples only in December 1943, and attained a total production of some 1000 vehicles. A partly armored version of the tractor was used as a supply vehicle or a self-propelled mount for the 3.7 cm Flak 43. To replace the 15 cm *Panzerwerfer* 42 launcher on the "Maultier" chassis, a fully armored Heavy *Wehrmacht* Tractor was used to carry the 15 cm ten-barrel fog launcher.

The same vehicle became a self-propelled mount for the 3.7 cm Flak 43. The pictures show it in marching and firing trim.

This armored version of the "Heavy *Wehrmacht* Tractor" served to replace the "armored launcher" on Opel "Maultier" chassis, carrying the tenfold 15 cm fog launcher.

The Tatra Type "T 809" developed in Czechoslovakia was a successor to the "Heavy *Wehrmacht* Tractor."

Light *Wehrmacht* Tractor

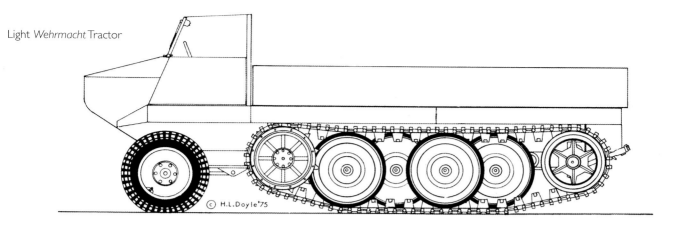

Heavy *Wehrmacht* Tractor

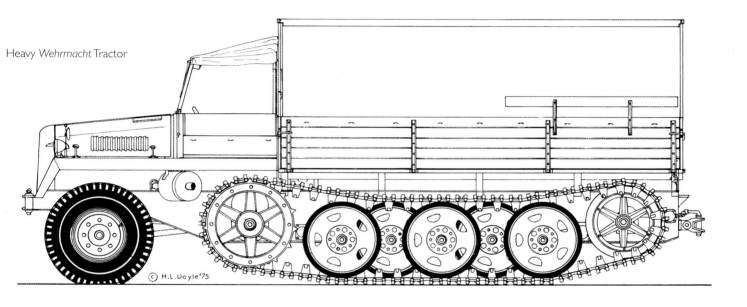

Heavy *Wehrmacht* Tractor (sWS), armored version.

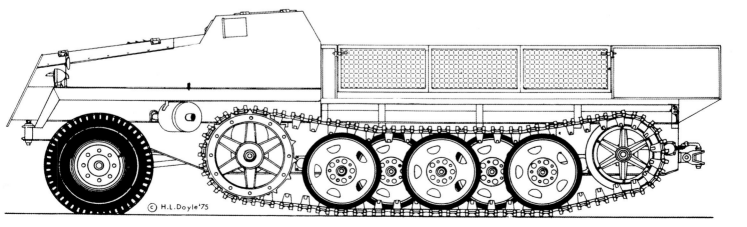

51

The further development of the "Heavy *Wehrmacht* Tractor" took place after the war's end in Czechoslovakia, where leftover components were used up. In 1953 Tatra fitted one of these vehicles with an air-cooled 12-cylinder Diesel engine, which served as the prototype for the Type "T 809" of 1955. This vehicle was powered by a 140 HP air-cooled V8 Diesel engine of about ten-liter displacement. Its payload was eight tons, its ground pressure some 0.6 kg/sq. cm. Series production did not take place.

The "Maultier" Series

The rough demands of the Russian theater of war created almost insurmountable difficulties for the supply troops. The German Army's wheeled vehicles were simply not able to meet these demands. Since most troop supplying was done with the standard three-ton truck of the "Fast Program," it was vital to make these vehicles better able to meet demand. A *Waffen*-SS development involved a Carden-Lloyd chassis, which was now considered for use on the three-ton truck. This development was designated "Maultier" (Mule). Normal rear-drive trucks had their rear axles replaced by a simple tracked running gear. The front axle was kept. The payload dropped to two tons, and these vehicles were designated "Tracked Truck two-ton, open (Maultier) (Sd.Kfz. 3)." The Opel firm used the Type 3.6-36 S with gasoline motors and Kloeckner-Humboldt-Deutz used the Type "S 3000" with Diesel motors, while the Ford Works rebuilt their Type "G 398 TS/V 3000 S."

Hitler agreed to have a total of 1870 complete "Maultier" trucks delivered as of 31 December 1942. The rebuilding of the remaining 2130 trucks at the front was to be checked by the Quartermaster General. It was to be determined whether the work could not be done by flying columns in the army's front areas.

The *Wehrmacht* called for 8500 trucks by 1 May 1943. The vehicles were to be replaced as of 1 June 1943 by a newer type. In fact 636 vehicles were built in 1942, and 13,000 in 1943, while production sank to 7310 in 1944. Opel produced about 4000 of these

At the beginning of "Maultier" development, the drive axle remained in its original position. The tracks were mounted in swinging form. This picture shows a Ford truck towing a light 10.5 cm howitzer.

A similar vehicle is being demonstrated in heavy country.

The production version of the most often built "Tracked Truck two-ton" (Sd.Kfz. 3), of which Ford produced some 14,000.

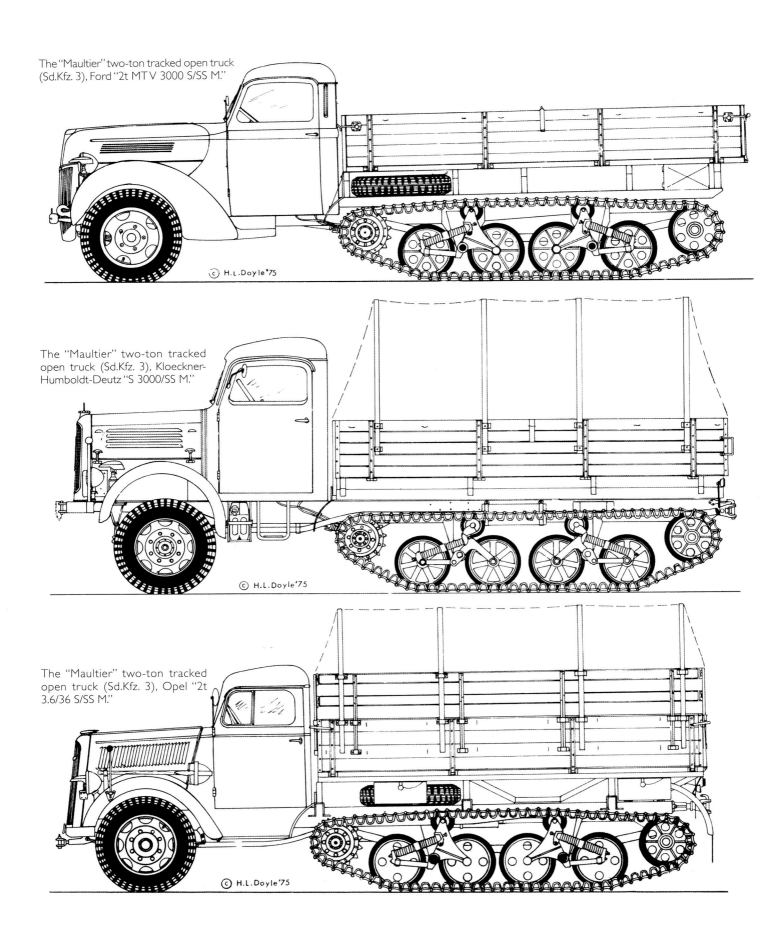

The "Maultier" two-ton tracked open truck (Sd.Kfz. 3), Ford "2t MTV 3000 S/SS M."

© H.L.Doyle '75

The "Maultier" two-ton tracked open truck (Sd.Kfz. 3), Kloeckner-Humboldt-Deutz "S 3000/SS M."

© H.L.Doyle '75

The "Maultier" two-ton tracked open truck (Sd.Kfz. 3), Opel "2t 3.6/36 S/SS M."

© H.L.Doyle '75

54

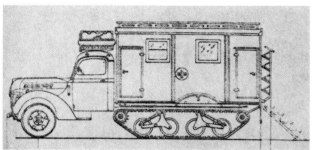

Opel supplied the troops with about 4000 "Maultier" vehicles. Only rear-drive "S" types were considered for this rebuilding.

The pictures at right, from top to bottom, show that these vehicles were also rebuilt in makeshift form as self-propelled mounts. The picture shows a Ford truck carrying a 2 cm Flak gun.

In rare cases, the closed uniform *Wehrmacht* bodies were also used, usually as ambulances.

The Kloeckner-Humboldt-Deutz version was the only "Maultier" type fitted with a Diesel motor. By the Führer's order, the "Maultier" name was dropped as of 27 March 1944.

Kloeckner-Humboldt-Deutz built some 2500 of these units (above and below).

Sometimes the road wheels were made as full-disc wheels. The running gear had been developed by the *Waffen-SS*.

How confusing anniversary figures could be is shown by these pictures.

55

vehicles, Ford about 14,000, while Kloeckner-Humboldt-Deutz contributed some 2500 units.

The French auto industry took part in this building program. Among others, the French Ford works in Asnieres built 1000 of these vehicles. The majority of the "Maultier" were delivered with open bodywork, but a few used the uniform box body of the German *Wehrmacht*.

Some "Maultier" vehicles were used with 2 cm Flak 38 guns by the anti-aircraft troops.

In 1942 the Opel firm began to design a simplified tracked running gear, a complete self-contained component that could be

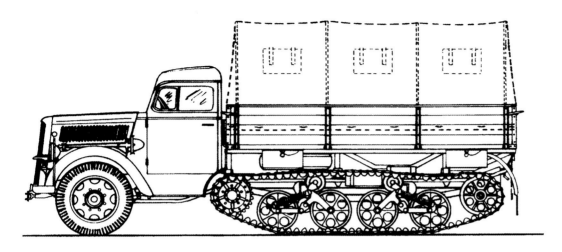

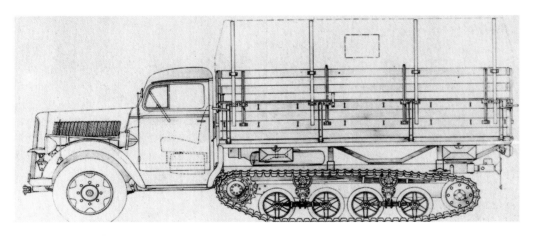

The two drawings compare the original running gear with the design proposed by the Opel firm.

A truck with Opel running gear is being tested while towing a trailer.

installed on any three-ton Type "S" truck or removed from it in a very short time.

The running gear was no longer bolted fast to the truck's frame, but attached to the normal rear springs. The front part was attached by quarter-elliptic springs to the existing transverse frame member.

While in the first tests the existing rear axle in its original position supplied power unchanged and the entire running gear was mounted around the axle, free to swing, the driveshaft was then shortened. The existing rear axle of the Opel three-ton "S" type with 6:41 reduction, but without rubber-tired wheels, was used. In their place,

The picture shows the Opel running gear ready for installation on an Opel Blitz truck.

The drawing shows the simple removal of the Opel running gear, which could be attached to any three-ton chassis without costing much time.

The finished vehicle with its tracked rear running gear.

The "15 cm *Panzerwerfer* 43" (Sd.Kfz. 4/1) used the Opel "Maultier" chassis in its original form. The armor thickness was 8 mm. 300 of these vehicles were built.

recessed forged track-drive wheels with a diameter of 460 mm and sixteen teeth were used. The tracks were the same as those of the Panzer I. Leaf springs, which could be repaired or replaced by simple means by the troops, and were used exclusively to suspend the running gear. A hydraulic auxiliary brake operated on both rear brakes, which could be used to brake the individual tracks. The Opel tracked running gear was designed from the ground up for installation on a truck chassis. With its low weight compared with earlier designs, it provided a very high degree of sturdiness.

In January 1943 Hitler decided that the SS version of the three-ton "Maultier" would continue to be built. At first, production was to number 1000 units per month. A further increase was to be striven for quickly, along with the increased production of the three-ton "S" type.

The Opel development, though, was to be halted. If the SS version was to cause previously unseen problems, the Opel vehicle could be built again. The SS führer, who had developed the SS version, was to receive a reward of 50,000 Reichsmark from Hitler. The SS "Reich" Division took part in the development.

Three hundred of the original vehicles were fitted with light armored bodies and the 15 cm ten-barreled Fog Launcher 41, which could rotate 360 degrees. Additional orders called for another 300 vehicles as ammunition carriers. Ninety of them were on hand on 1 August 1943.

In addition, 300 ammunition carriers of this type were built and used as supply vehicles.

The 15 cm *Panzerwerfer* 43 launcher (Sd.Kfz. 4/1)

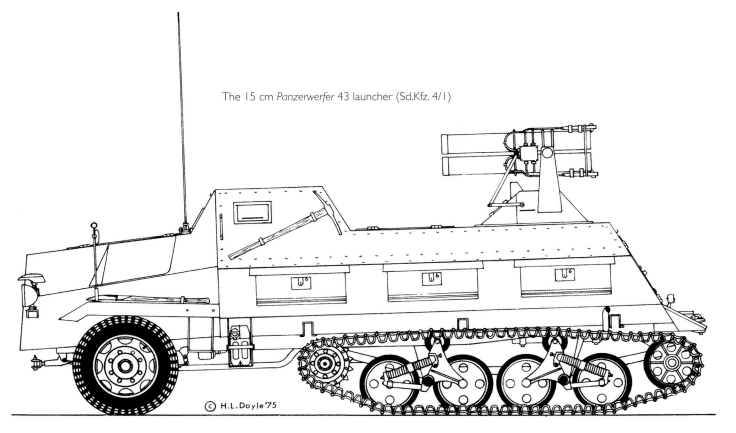

© H.L.Doyle '75

A 4.5 ton "Maultier" vehicle was to be hastily developed and quickly prepared for testing. It was to be used mainly as a towing vehicle for the Pak 43. Daimler-Benz and Buesing-NAG turned in suggestions for it. Daimler-Benz received an initial contract for 600 vehicles. Series production was to begin in May 1943. After the rear axle of the 4.5-ton "S" truck, a complete "Panzer II" tracked running gear unit was installed. Weaknesses in the drive train cast doubts as to this vehicle's use for towing, so it was used chiefly as a supply truck. The first 40 vehicles were delivered in August 1943, and 594 of the "Tracked Truck 4.5-ton open (Maultier)" in all were built in that year. Another 886 units followed in 1944. Since the top speed of the "Maultier" vehicles of 20 to 25 kph was quite sufficient, experiments were to be made to see if a reduction gear could be installed to protect the gearbox.

The Daimler-Benz AG, much like Opel, developed a very simplified tracked running gear for this vehicle; it was to be used after the "Panzer II" running gear went out of production. Only a few prototypes of it were built. The development of these vehicles took place at the Gaggenau works.

Of the 4.5-ton version of the "Maultier" series, there was just this one version from the Daimler-Benz AG. The pictures show the vehicle with the original cab, and the "uniform" cab used later on all trucks in the German *Wehrmacht*.

On 8 July 1944, on account of the fuel situation, Hitler again urged an energetic effort to use Diesel engines in trucks, tractors, and tanks, as well as their series production with all possible haste. Thus, as of 1943 the development of a rebuilding kit for the common Opel six-cylinder truck was already begun. Water-cooling was to be given up, but the present production was to continue, interchangeability assured, and a break in production avoided. But it turned out that a purely air-cooled machine required a different arrangement of cylinders. This in turn was impossible because of the available machine tools. Instead of air-cooling the whole motor, oil cooling for the cylinders and air-cooling for the cylinder heads was suggested. The main parts of the water-cooled motor could be retained, with only an air blower and an additional oil pump added.

Here too, the running gear was to be simplified greatly. The upper picture shows the lowered device similar to the Opel running gear, which could be installed on any 4.5-ton "S" truck as a separate unit.

This view of the vehicle shows the auxiliary frame of the running gear and the clearly simple attachment of it to the existing chassis.

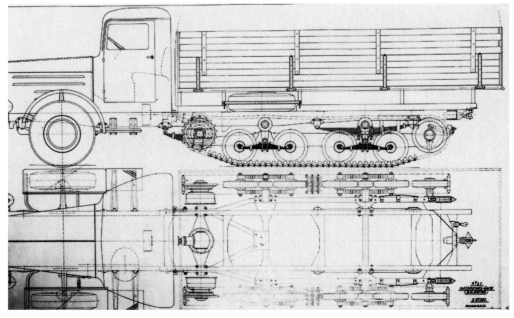

Buessing-NAG also tried to take part in this development, but could only make suggestions.

Along with the gasoline motor, a Diesel process with a Lanova combustion system was also tested. A conference at the Führer's headquarters on 6 November 1944 resulted in further development of the "OM 302" water-cooled Diesel engine developed by Daimler-Benz at Gaggenau for the three-ton truck. In view of the task that the newly formed sub-commission of the EKK had been given regarding the conversion of the 3-t-A truck made by Opel into an antitank-gun towing vehicle, though, the air-cooled six-cylinder "OM 175" motor had to be developed further. The experimental department of the Daimler-Benz AG was to build ten more "OM 175" motors, half using the DB eddy chamber and half with the MAN combustion chamber.

For the vehicles of the 4.5-ton class, air-cooling was originally not required. But to be prepared for such a request, the Daimler-Benz AG developed an air-cooled six-cylinder "OM 67/6" Diesel engine, which, fitted with the DB eddy chamber, had shown good performance on the test bench and in road testing with an axial blower. To save weight, though, and because of the no longer modern design, the "OM 176" was to be preferred to the "OM 67/6." All of this development had not been completed when the war ended. In this respect, it ought to be learned under what prerequisites the

production basis of the 12-cylinder air-cooled Tatra "103" motor could be essentially extended.

The 8-ton Halftrack and HK 900 Series

On 20 July 1932, a conference on the development program had taken place at Leiter Wa Prw, dealing with, among others, the development of towing tractors. Then-Major Nehring expressed the wishes of In. 4 there, explaining that there was no immediate urgent need for a medium towing machine, but an urgent need for a heavy towing machine. General Karlewski, who was present, objected that the existing solution to transporting the existing medium calibers could only be regarded as an extremely makeshift matter that would be totally insufficient for the future P-guns because of their heavier weights. As an artilleryman, he could not get along without the further development of a medium towing machine that was fully usable both on and off the road. Which towing machine, the medium or the heavy type, was more urgent he could not say. This decision would be needless anyway, as the development of the heavy towing machine was already much farther along. Delaying the development of the medium towing machine even further

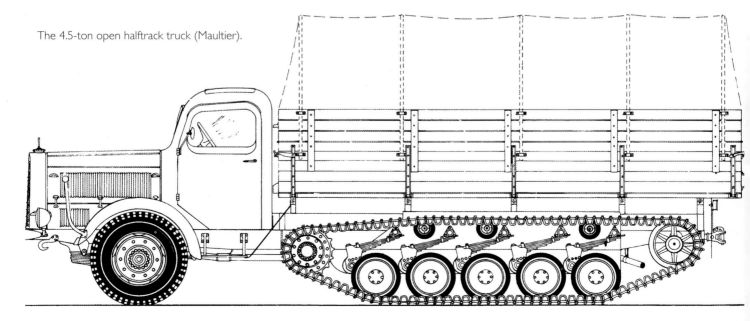

The 4.5-ton open halftrack truck (Maultier).

The first production version of the medium off-road towing vehicle made by the Krauss-Maffei AG was this 1934 type with short tracks.

Right: The "KM m 8" version built in 1934 and 1935 was built by Daimler-Benz and Buessing-NAG, as well as Krauss-Maffei.

The vehicles were used mainly to tow the 7.5 cm 16n.A. field cannon, which was loaded onto a sprung one-axle trailer for this purpose (below).

The lower left picture shows the loading of a gun onto a trailer.

was, he believed, not bearable. The further discussion concluded that the design and building of the heavy towing machine should be completed quickly, and the development of the medium towing machine should be carried on at the previous speed.

The Krauss-Maffei AG of Munich-Allach was responsible for the development of the medium towing machine. As already noted, it had been occupied with the production of various types of towing vehicles since the thirties.

It produced the first version developed by the Army Weapons Office in 1934. The first production version, which followed the usual design trends of the times, had comparatively short tracks with just four road wheels. It was assigned mainly to artillery units, where it towed field guns loaded onto two-wheeled trailers. Toward the end of 1934 it was replaced by the 1934 type of the medium off-road-capable towing vehicle (Sd.Kfz. 7), which now had a five-wheel running gear. The vehicle was still powered by the Maybach "HL 52" six-cylinder, 115 HP powerplant, and with a gross weight of 11 tons it had a listed pulling power of 8000 kp. Included in this series were the Kraus-Maffei (Type KM m 8) vehicles (chassis no. 8002 and 8008), the Daimler-Benz version (Type DB m 8, chassis no. 17055-17059), and the Buessing-NAG vehicles (Type BN m 8) with chassis numbers 20001 to 20010. They were still equipped with Ross steering. In the Krauss-Maffei version, the hand-brake lever worked on the mechanical brakes of the vehicle through chassis number 802. Krauss-Maffei produced 380 units of this version.

In 1935 and 1936, the successor type "KM m 9" was built only by Kraus-Maffei. Now the Maybach "HL 57" motor was installed. The vehicles were intended mainly to tow the heavy Field Howitzer 18, the heavy 10 cm Cannon, and the 8.8 cm Flak gun. Eleven men could be carried on the vehicle; 127 of them were built by Krauss-Maffei.

The Type "KM m 10," which appeared at the end of 1936, was built just like its predecessor, but had the Maybach "HL 62" motor installed. This type was also built by the Hansa-Lloyd-Goliath Works in Bremen and designated "HL m 10." The first series was still equipped with ZF Ross steering, while the second series of Types "HL m 10" and "KM m 10" were fitted with the Muenz Type 4 steering. In all, Hansa-Lloyd-Goliath produced 22 of these vehicles, which were built until 1937. Production at Krauss-Maffei numbered 11 units.

The final version of this series, the Type "KM m 11," was built from 1937 to 1945. The number of road wheels in the running gear had risen from four to six, and the tracks were now 2235 mm long. The gross weight had risen to 11.55 tons. As before, there were eleven seats. Hansa-Lloyd-Goliath (later Borgward) took part in production, with the type designation "HL m 11." From 1943 on, Krauss-Maffei increased its monthly production to 100 units and built a total of 5025 of the "KM m 11" vehicles.

The total number of eight-ton towing vehicles (Sd.Kfz. 7) in the *Wehrmacht* reached 3262 units at the end of 1942. In 1943 3251 towing vehicles of this size were built; in 1944, another 3298. In all, some 12,000 of these vehicles were produced, of which 6120 came from the patenting firm of Krauss-Maffei.

The :KM m 8" vehicle towing the 15 cm sFH 18 howitzer.

The Krauss-Maffei prototype "KM 7," December 1933.

The "KM m 9" and "KM m 10" vehicles differed only in the installed motor. Externally, the two vehicles were identical. This picture shows the original version of the front fenders.

The pictures of the chassis show the changed fenders and the main components of the chassis.

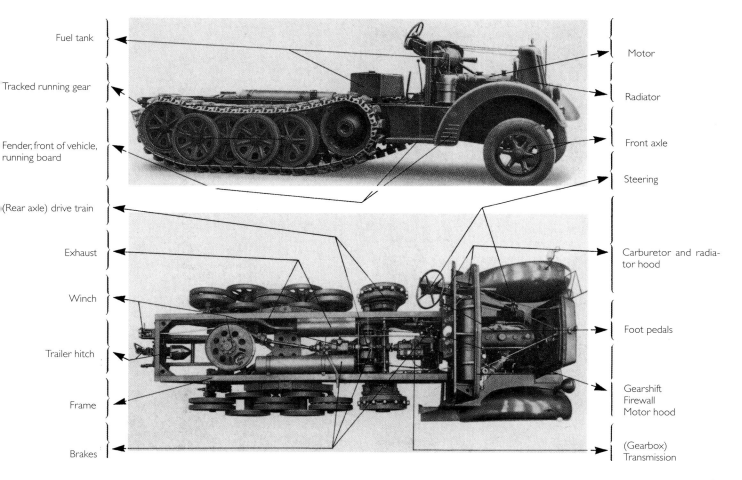

Fuel tank

Tracked running gear

Fender, front of vehicle, running board

(Rear axle) drive train

Exhaust

Winch

Trailer hitch

Frame

Brakes

Motor

Radiator

Front axle

Steering

Carburetor and radiator hood

Foot pedals

Gearshift
Firewall
Motor hood

(Gearbox)
Transmission

Eight-ton towing vehicles were used to tow low-loader trailers (Sd.Anh. 115) to recover tanks (above).

From top to bottom: The Type "KM m 11" was built in large series until 1945. The picture shows finished vehicles at Krauss-Maffei in Munich.

To the left, next to "KM m 11" chassis, are completed "KM m 8" vehicles, including an unusual type with the rear body of a truck.

The Type "KM m 11" was most often used to tow the 8.8 cm Flak gun. This one is being used by the Luftwaffe.

The rear view of the "KM m 11" vehicle shows the storage space for ammunition and tools.

Examples of the development of Sd.Kfz. 7:
Above: KMZ 85/100, April 1933
Below: KMZ 100, February 1934

The Maybach "HL 62 TUK" motor with gearbox, seen from the carburetor (above) and exhaust (below) sides.

It was typical for the front axles of halftrack vehicles to lift in rough terrain.

A test drive in deep snow.

The closing compartments held not only tools, but also equipment and supplies (lower left).

The final version of Sd. Kfz. 7.

The ZF gearbox seen from the side and from below.

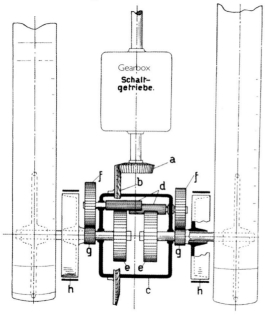

Gearbox
**Schalt-
getriebe.**

This drawing shows the steering drive used on all towing vehicles.
The drive-wheel drive of the medium towing vehicle.

The arrangement of the running gear with the road wheels removed shows their suspension by leaf springs and the crank arms that hold the wheels.

The bolts marked a) prevented any overburdening of the tracked running gear by breaking. The picture shows details of the leading-wheel crank arm and the track-tightening apparatus.

This picture shows details of the greased track links.

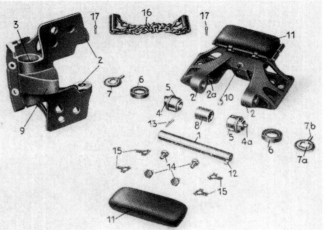

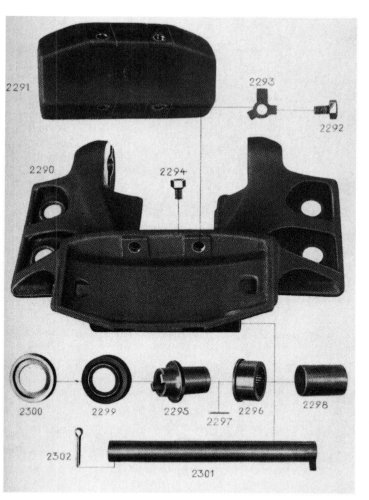

The construction of the tracks.

By May 1941, FIAT had finished a prototype of a halftrack vehicle based on a German model, and reserved this Type "727" for negotiations with German firms because of a license to make "Richter" tracks. The drawings for the towing-machine tracks were delivered to FIAT during 1942. They were intended for use with the "727" and "Dovunque 41" types. The Type "727" had a load limit of 1.5 tons and a top speed of 53 kph. The listed towing power was six tons. The vehicle was ordered in June 1943, and was to reach the troops by April 1944. Its inherent weight was three tons.

Components of a track link: 2291. Rubber pad with holder, 2290. Track link, 2294. Oil-chamber closing screw, 2300. Securing disc, 2299, Sliding thickener, 2295. Inner bearing box, 2296. Outer bearing box, 2298. Spacing box, 2301. Track-link bolt (upper left picture).

The standard body of the eight-ton towing machine (below).

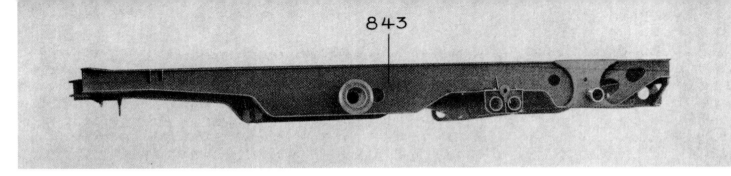

The frame of the eight-ton towing machine.

The attachment of the trailer hitch.
1. Hitch-swinging lock
2. Hitch removal lock
3. Hitching bolt
4. Bolt lock

Details of the winch installed in the frame.
1. Shift lever for reduction and winch
2. Two-piece driveshaft
3. Clutch lever
4. Lower cable drum
5. Oil filler screw
6. Gearshift lever
7.

The second vehicle was a variant of the six-wheel "Dovunque" vehicle made by SPA. A halftrack vehicle was supposed to be developed from it on the basis of experience gained with Type "727."

A five-ton payload was planned for this vehicle, and its top speed was 50 kph. The building of prototypes began at the start of 1943. The Type "Dovunque 42" followed, with a 3.5-ton payload and a top speed of up to 68 kph. This development was interrupted by the armistice in September 1943. These vehicles too were never put into production.

The BREDA firm copied the "KM m 11" vehicle almost unchanged; externally, only the radiator grille and engine hood, as well as the right-hand drive, were noticeable. This Type "61," though, was

Below: Attaching snow chains to the rubber pads of the tracks.

Below: A towing vehicle made by FIAT in Turin, with the running gear of the eight-ton towing machine. Only prototypes were built.

fitted with the BREDA "T 14" six-cylinder, 130 HP gasoline engine. From 1943 on, several hundred units were produced for the German *Wehrmacht*. Later BREDA limited itself to producing replacement parts. The possibility of using the vehicles as self-propelled mounts for a 7.5 cm Cannon L/46 or 9 cm Cannon L/53 was also explored. They were to be used as antitank weapons.

Toward the end of the war, the Austrian Saurerwerke AG of Vienna also took part in this production. With an average completion time of 15 months, a towing machine was priced at 36,000 Reichsmark. In 1942, Henschel had produced twenty of these units for testing. The bodies for the eight-ton towing machine came mainly from the firms of Jessen in Hamburg and Lindner in Ammendorf.

The Breda Type "61" differed from the "KM m 11" vehicle in having a different radiator grille and motor (upper left).

Compared with the "KM m 11" chassis, only the right-hand steering is different. The vehicle was only produced in small numbers (above).

Left: The Sd.Kfz. 7/1 carried a 2 cm Flak quad and towed an Sd.Anh. 56 trailer.

The side walls of the gun platform could be folded down flat in action to increase the crew's freedom of movement (below).

As Sd.Kfz. 7/1, the vehicle was used as a self-propelled mount for the 2 cm Flak Quad 38 in Mount 400. The self-propelled mount carried the guns, parts of the gun equipment, and the entire crew, consisting of the driver, gun leader, and four men. Six hundred rounds of ready ammunition were carried. The rest of the equipment and ammunition were loaded on an Sd.Anh. 56 trailer. The gross weight of the vehicle was 11,540 kg. The weapon itself was soon provided with a shield, while the driver's and crew's seats were protected with armor plate only later, and then only partially. Some examples carried only a 2 cm Flak 30; this may have been a change made by the troops. The eight-ton chassis also carried the 3.7 cm Flak 36 and was then designated Sd.Kfz. 7/2. With a

A comparison of Sd.Kfz. 7/1 and 7/2.

The Sd.Kfz. 7/2 with the 3.7 cm Flak 36 and armor-plated cab and radiator (upper right).

The final version had rear walls made of wood (right).

The experimental installation of a 5 cm Flak 41 on an eight-ton towing machine. The braces attached to the sides of the vehicle had to be swung out for action (below).

Below Right: Sd.Kfz. 7/6 as a Flak ranging-troop truck, with a special body for twelve men.

seven-man crew, the vehicle had a fighting weight of 11,050 kg. Even as towing vehicles, several of the units were armored for protection as the superiority of the Allied air forces became more and more obvious. For the anti-aircraft troops, an aircraft ranging truck (Sd.Kfz. 7/6) was built to carry a 13-man crew. It was also the anti-aircraft artillery that mounted a 5 cm Flak 41 gun on this chassis experimentally. When being fired, though, four braces had to steady the truck because of the gun's heavy weight. Since its readiness to fire was thus limited considerably, the development of this vehicle was not continued. V-2 rocket units were assigned

An Sd.Kfz. 7 as a fire-control vehicle for "V-2" rocket units. The launching pad for the rocket is at the rear.

The vehicle was backed into the firing position, so that observations of the shot could be made under armor protection.

This picture shows the firing position of a "V-2" rocket with the Meiller transport trailer and the fire-control vehicle.

eight-ton towing machines in 1944 as fire-control vehicles. They were also used to tow launching platforms. After the war ended, the British occupation forces acquired thirty "KM m 11" vehicles in September and October 1945.

The simultaneous development of the "HK 900" series carried on by Kraus-Maffei in 1940 created prototypes designated "HK. 901." They were intended to replace the five- and eight-ton medium towing wagons. Buessing-NAG of Berlin-Oberschoeneweide was also involved in the development. With a total weight of 9.5 tons, they were to reach a top speed of 50 kph. A 155 HP Maybach "HL 66" motor was intended for installation. A noticeable feature of this

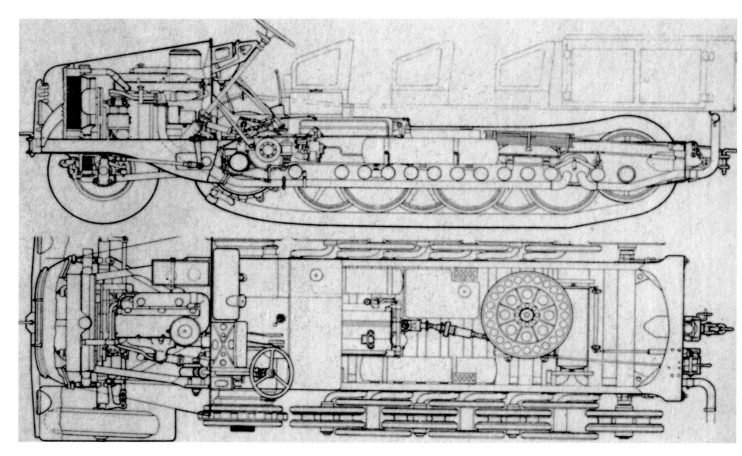

This drawing shows a test vehicle of the "HK 900" series, the Type "HK 904."

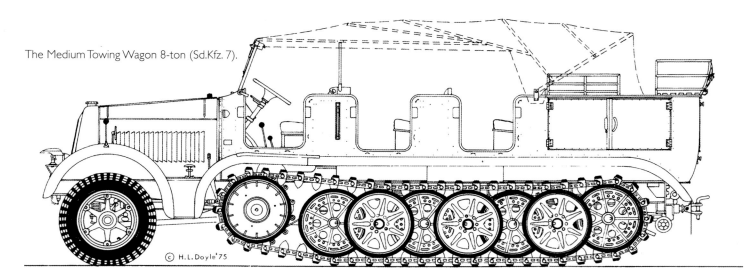

The Medium Towing Wagon 8-ton (Sd.Kfz. 7).

© H.L.Doyle '75

series was the use of torsion bars as springs for the tracked running gear, for until then, only leaf springs had been used for the eight-ton series. Maybach OLVAR gearboxes made shifting easier. After four prototypes had been built, a zero series of another thirty vehicles was approved. These thirty vehicles were divided into fifteen Type "HK.904" with OLVAR transmissions and fifteen Type "HK.905" with OLVAT transmissions and uniform running gear.

The keen interest of foreign countries in the German towing-machine development is shown by the fact that these vehicles were also built in Britain. By contract from the Ministry of Supply, the Vauxhall Motors firm of Luton, Bedfordshire, built six prototypes of the "BT" vehicle, an exact copy of the German eight-ton towing

machine, in 1944-45. Since available powerplants had to be used, each vehicle was fitted with two production 214 cubic inch gasoline truck motors. The tests were given up at the war's end.

12-ton halftrack and HK.1601 series vehicles

Based on the experience gained from the "Marienwagen," the Daimler-Benz AG of Berlin-Marienfelde developed the "ZD.5" halftrack towing vehicle in 1931-32. The 9.3-ton vehicle had rear-driven tracks. The twelve-cylinder, 150 HP Maybach "DSO 8" motor was installed. The firm carried out the project for Russian customers. The vehicles, like other German military vehicles, were actually tested continually in Russia. Daimler-Benz was already trying in vain to

Even in England a test was undertaken to copy German halftrack vehicles. The picture shows the model of the 1844-45 "BYT" vehicle built by Vauxhall Motors.

Six of these vehicles were built, each equipped with two Bedford truck motors. When the war ended, this development was halted.

In 1931-32 the Daimler-Benz AG delivered several Type "ZD 5" vehicles to Russia. They were the forerunners of the later twelve-ton towing machine series. The picture shows the chassis with rear drive wheels. The front axle had rubber tires.

Right: The front view of the "ZD 5" shows the unusual suspension of the front wheels.

Below: The side view shows the front suspension with load equalization to the tracked running gear. The body already corresponds to later conceptions.

The first production model of the Type "DB s 7" 12-ton heavy towing wagon (Sd.Kfz. 8) appeared in 1934. Here it is towing the 15 cm sFH 18 howitzer.

The vehicle was almost always used as an artillery tractor for heavy guns.

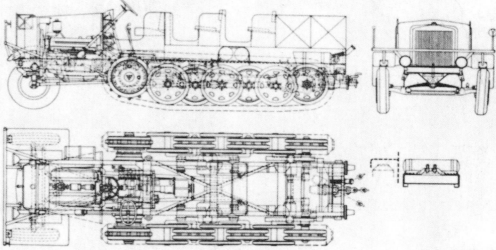

The Type "DB s 8" followed in 1936, and was still equipped with the Maybach "DSO 8" motor. The vehicle now had the uniform radiator grille used on other types of towing machines.

The production model "DB 9" is seen during off-road testing. The visual profile of the vehicle could be lessened considerably by folding down the windshield.

The "DB 9" vehicle is pulling a heavy gun. This vehicle had not only excellent towing performance, but also sufficient off-road capability.

The driver's seat of the "DB 10," with the rubber padding of the drive wheel easy to see. The crew's shelter from the weather was insufficient.

The final version of the 12-ton towing machine appeared in 1939 and had sheet-steel front wheels instead of the formerly customary cast steel, spoked type.

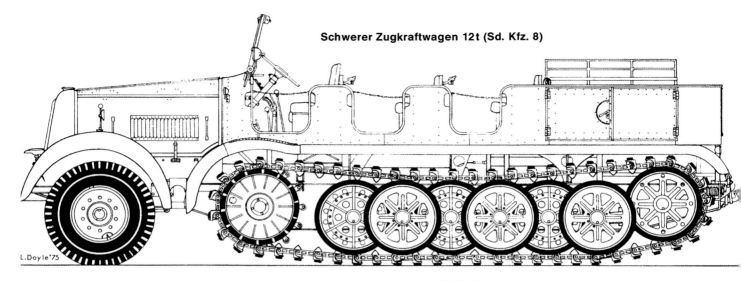

Schwerer Zugkraftwagen 12t (Sd. Kfz. 8)

L.Doyle '75

Twelve-ton Heavy Towing Wagon (Sd.Kfz. 8)

Two of the 17 cm Cannon 18 in mortar mounts were towed by a 12-ton towing machine.

Starting the vehicle with a crank starter: 1. Oil bath air filter, 2. Cloth cover for the air intakes not needed for starting, 3. Acetylene generator, 4. Cover, 5. Hand crank, 6. Handle for starter.

The vehicles were also fitted with front plows for snow and obstacle removal: 1. Coupling 2. Snowplow.

Tracked "MSZ 201" vehicle made by the Maffei firm.

One-ton light towing wagon (Sd.Kfz. 10).

Three-ton light towing wagon (Sd.Kfz. 11).

Eight-ton medium towing wagon (Sd.Kfz. 7).

Heavy *Wehrmacht* Tractor (sWS).

18-ton heavy towing wagon (Sd.Kfz. 9).

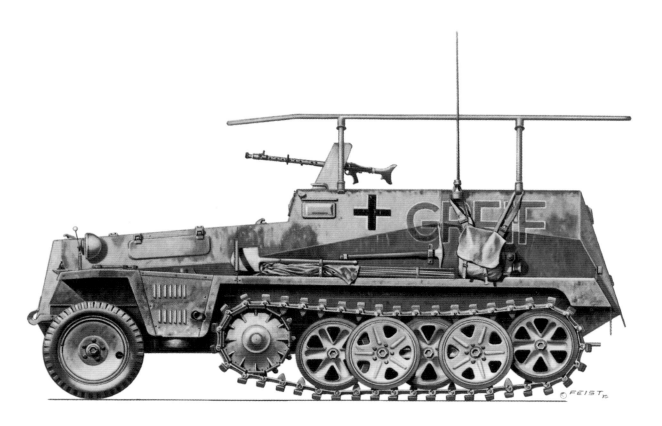

Light armored radio truck (Sd.Kfz. 250/3).

Medium armored troop carrier (Sd.Kfz. 251).

Years after the war ended, the Czech People's Army used 12-ton towing vehicles built in their country to tow heavy Russian guns.

break the Maybach motor monopoly, and suggested the use of the eight-cylinder DB "M 07" motor. In 1934, according to the guidelines of the Army Weapons Office, the Type "DB s7" appeared; it was introduced to the troops as the "heavy off-road-capable towing wagon (Sd.Kfz. 8) Type 1934. Its weight had risen to 14.4 tons; its listed pulling power was 12 tons. An improved version of this towing vehicle was introduced in 1936 as Type "DB s8." It was used to tow the 21 cm mortar, the 15 cm K. 16, and the 10.5 cm Flak gun. As before, it used the Maybach "DSO 8" motor. The vehicle remained in production until 1938, at which time it was replaced by a further improved type, the "DB 9." Unchanged in appearance, it now had the Maybach "HL 85" gasoline engine installed. The gross weight

was now 15 tons; it could carry thirteen men and an 800-kg payload, and its towing power increased to 14 tons. Repeated attempts by Daimler-Benz to have the Army Weapons Office allow the use of the DB "OM 48/1" Diesel engine failed. In October 1939 the final version of the series appeared, the Type "DB 10." Visible features of this type were the use of sheet-steel disc wheels in place of the usual cast spoked type. The price of a vehicle was 46,000 Reichsmark. It usually towed the 15 cm K. 16 gun-barrel vehicle, the 15 cm K. 16 mount vehicle, the 15 cm K. 16 as a load carrier, the 15 cm K. 18 in similar manner, the 10.5 cm Flak, and the 21 cm mortar. On 22 October 1939 there were apparently twelve 8.8 cm self-propelled Flak mounts based on the 12-ton towing wagon in use.

The 18-ton Heavy Towing Vehicle (Sd.Kfz. 9).

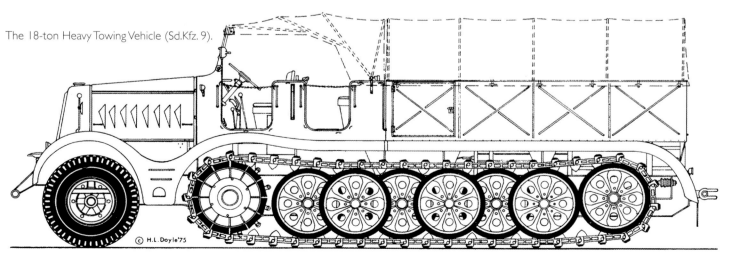

The Friedrich Krupp AG of Muelhausen, Alsace, and firms in Czechoslovakia took part in building these vehicles. The Czech Army was still using these vehicles in the fifties. On 20 December 1942 there were 1615 of these towing machines is use by the German *Wehrmacht*. In 1943 507 more were built, while 602 were produced in 1944. Of the roughly 4000 12-ton vehicles that were built, the Krauss-Maffei AG works delivered 315 in 1940 and 1941.

The final version of the 12-ton series appeared in 1941 as Type "HK. 1601." It was supposed to replace the 12- and 18-ton towing machines. This vehicle weighed 16.2 tons, and was powered by the six-cylinder, 300 HP Maybach "HL 116" motor. It had a top speed of 67.5 kph and a towing power of 16 tons. 34 of these vehicles were ordered for presumed delivery in February 1941. They were designated "HK. 1604," and the prototypes were developed by Daimler-Benz and Famo.

18-ton Halftrack Series

The heaviest type included in German towing-machine development was the "Heavy Towing Wagon 18 ton (Sd.Kfz. 9)" developed and built by the "Fahrzeug- und Motorenbau GmbH (FAMO)" in Breslau. Its development began in 1935 and resulted in the Type "FM gr 1" in 1936, an 18-ton heavy towing vehicle for a total road-train weight of 35.5 tons. The vehicle was used mainly to tow the 24 cm Cannon 3, which was developed by Krupp and introduced in 1937. Its price was 75,000 Reichsmark. The improved "F 2" version

The only known variant of the 12-ton towing vehicle carried an 8.8 cm Flak 18 gun (1940).

Daimler-Benz and Famo collaborated in 1941 on replacing the 12- and 18-ton towing vehicles. A uniform vehicle was supposed to replace both types. This picture shows the "HK. 1601," which was to be considered, but only prototypes were built.

with the 250 HP Maybach "HL 98" motor appeared in 1938 with a lowered price of 60,000 RM per unit, thanks to higher production quantities. The vehicles were intended for towing low loaders with total weights of up to 35 tons, and for this purpose they had a divided rear body for crew and payload. They often saw service in tank-recovery units, where they were highly appreciated. During the war, most of the vehicles in use were fitted with a rear spur, which increased the performance of the motor winch. After the heavy "Panther" and "Tiger" tanks were introduced, up to three of these vehicles had to be used to recover one tank.

924

The 18-ton towing vehicle developed by FAMO, and also built later by Vomag and Tatra, was the heaviest type in the German towing-machine series. This picture shows the final "F 3" variety as a tank-recovery vehicle.

In off-road use, the front wheels often lifted completely off the ground, and the vehicle's load rested entirely on the tracked running gear.

The body developed for tank-recovery work was also used to carry replacement parts and towing equipment of all kinds.

After the "Panther" and "Tiger" tanks were introduced the towing power was no longer enough, and sometimes up to three 18-ton towing machines were needed to tow one tank.

As long as Panzer III and IV had to be serviced, these vehicles towed 22-ton low loaders (Sd.Anh. 116).

To heighten the towing power of the winch line, massive spurs were installed on the vehicles used to recover heavy tanks. The spurs often varied in appearance.

To tow the heaviest artillery, such as the 24 cm Cannon 3, the Sd.Kfz. 9 was fitted with the usual artillery body, which not only offered space for the gun crew, but also held a quantity of readiness ammunition.

From top to bottom: Chassis of the 18-ton towing wagon made by FAMO are seen in various phases of assembly.

Here the frame is being welded together.

The torsion bars are connected to the crank arms of the running gear.

The final "F 3" type appeared in 1939 and was built by FAMO in Breslau until shortly before the war ended.

The Vomag Maschinenfabrik AG in Plauen, Vogtland also produced Type "F 3" chassis in series as of 1940. Finally, the Ringhoffer-Tatra firm took part in producing these vehicles in the last years of the war. These towing wagons had undergone a series of simplifications to save raw materials and production time. Tatra also fitted the vehicles it built with the air-cooled 12-cylinder Type 103 Diesel motor. FAMO and Vomag continued to use the Maybach "HL 108" gasoline engine. The pulling power was still 18 tons.

On 20 December 1942 the Army had 855 of these important vehicles; 643 were built in 1943 and 834 in 1944. In all, some 2500 18-ton units were built.

The picture shows the staggered running gear with the drive wheel. The gearbox shows the drive to the winch, which can be seen at the far right.

The drive axle is being completed.

The sprung drive clutch is being installed.

Finally the parts of the body are added.

During the retreat combat of the last war years, these vehicles were also used to tow heavy ditch plows, in order to create needed field positions.

The 18-ton heavy towing vehicle is shown at the upper left with a six-ton swiveling crane (Sd.Kfz. 9/1).

The side view of this vehicle shows the crane built by the Bilstein firm. This vehicle was also used primarily by tank recovery units (above).

For heavy loads, a gasoline-electric powered ten-ton crane was used (center).

Before work on the Sd. Kfz. 9/2 began, the chassis had to be braced so as to eliminate the spring play of the suspension (bottom).

The Weserhuette firm mounted fourteen of these 8.8 cm Flak 37 (Sf) guns on 18-ton towing vehicles, but this combination did not work out well.

Artillery units used the 18-ton towing vehicle with a troop-carrying body to tow the Cannon 3, Mortar 1, and 12.8 cm Flak 40. As of 1943, the vehicle also served to tow a trench plow, which dug field defense lines quickly. The Bilstein firm of Altenvoerde received a contract on April 19, 1940, to create a "six-ton swiveling crane on an 18-ton heavy towing vehicle." It was to serve as a mobile lifting apparatus for tank workshop companies. The Sd.Kfz. 9/1 was introduced in September 1941. A stronger version with a gasoline-electric driven ten-ton crane was put into service later. This vehicle was designated "Sd.Kfz. 9/2." A 1942 requirement called for the building of 112 self-propelled mounts for the 8.8 cm Flak 37. In June and July 1943, fourteen of these "8.8 cm Flak 37 (Sf) on 18-ton towing vehicle" were actually delivered. But first, a strengthened torsion-bar suspension had to be installed, since the total weight had risen to 25 tons. The ammunition supply on board numbered 40 rounds. The motor and cab were covered with 14.5 mm armor. The vehicles were assembled at the Weserhuette in Bad Oeynhausen. On January 18, 1943, this version was declined as insufficient as a Flak gun by the *Luftwaffe*, and as an antitank gun by the Army. Within this series there was also a 1939 project designated "F 4" that existed only as plans. As with the "HK. 1601," the new six-cylinder Maybach "HL 116" motor was proposed for installation.

Also of interest is a development by FAMO, which designed a "Heavy Towing Vehicle" (V Kz 3501) in 1942. The 35-ton vehicle was meant for use as a towing tractor for heavy loads and towing work. The 650 HP Maybach "HL 210" was to be installed, giving the vehicle a top speed of 35 kph. Four vehicles were contracted for, with anticipated delivery in the spring of 1943. Unfortunately, no further data on this interesting design have been found.

The 1500 towing vehicles (1 to 18 tons) in Germany that needed repairs were totally overhauled and returned to the troops ready for use in a massive project that ended on October 15, 1944. On October 12, 1944, Speer reported that this project had been carried out, in which spare parts were exhausted and 1141 vehicles were overhauled and in use by the set date (1-ton: 302, 3-ton: 424, 5-ton: 91, 8-ton: 196, 12-ton: 57, and 18-ton: 71).

HL 100 Series

The towing vehicle for special loads in the mountains (such as grenade launchers, heavy machine guns, and field cables for telephones) called for by the Army Weapons Office in 1939 was patented as DRP 717 514, Kl. 63c, Gr. 30. The inventor was Engineer Heinrich Ernst Kniepkamp of Berlin-Charlottenburg. This new patent completed the array of motor vehicles with track drive and front running and steering wheels, with the steering gear, driver's seat, servicing elements, and running wheel arranged like those of a motorcycle. It was important that the only front running and steered wheel was located with its ground contact point at a distance from the foremost contact point of the tracks so that the wheel had sufficient steering effect through its ground pressure. The weight division within the vehicle ruled out nose-heaviness that would have hindered operation with the front steering wheel removed. The steering functioned via the familiar double-differential drive. The original patent was granted on June 29, 1939, and the development of the vehicle itself was carried out by the NSU AG in Neckarsulm. The powerplant was the 1.5 liter Opel "Olympia," which produced 36 HP. An additional radiator component became necessary, since the position of the motor behind the driver's seat did not allow direct cooling.

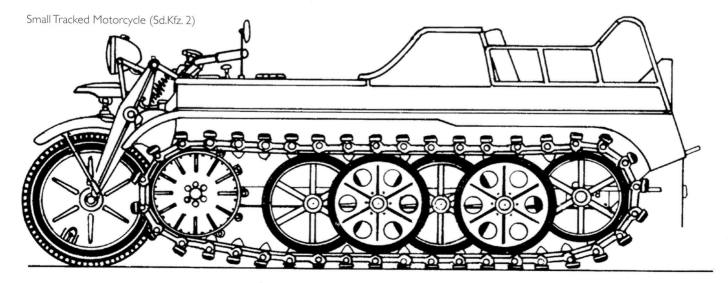

Small Tracked Motorcycle (Sd.Kfz. 2)

A contract was assigned to NSU for a 0 Series of 500 units, with projected delivery between July 1940 and the end of 1941. At this time the designation was "Tracked Vehicle, Narrow Towing Vehicle (HK. 101) (Sd.Kfz. 620)."

The General Army Communique No. 635 of June 5, 1941, mentions the official introduction of the vehicle to the troops. The small tracked vehicle was now no longer Test Vehicle 620, but Sd.Kfz. 2.

On December 20, 1942, there were 1208 units of the "Kettenkrad," as the troops called the vehicle, on hand; in 1943 the production rose to 2450, and in 1944 to 4490 units. Production plans for 1945 called for five hundred of the vehicles with single-axle trailers per month from the NSU Woprks AG, while Stoewer in Stettin was to produce 300 per month. But production suffered under the usual war conditions. Several French firms, including Simca, were supposed to be included in this production program. The NSU Works produced these vehicles after the war until 1948, and built 7813 of them in all.

To decrease ground pressure even more, tracks with widening plates could be used. The top speed with these tracks was not to go over 40 kph.

Known variants of the small tracked motorcycle include the small tracked cycle for phone cable (Sd.Kfz. 2/1) with a total weight of 1675 kg and a three-man crew, and the small tracked cycle for heavy phone cable (Sd.Kfz. 2/2), with a total weight of 1590 kg.

Small Tracked Motorcycle (Sd.Kfz. 2), this one from the 0 series delivered to the *Luftwaffe*, with a crew aboard.

The vehicle was originally planned as a towing vehicle for special loads in mountainous country. Here it is tested with a 7.5 cm Mountain Gun 36 in tow.

The "*Kettenkrad*" (tracked cycle) was basically delivered with a single-axle trailer. This version gave valuable service to all branches of the troops.

Above: The rear view of the vehicle shows the bench for the passengers. Below: For travel in roadless terrain, track-widening plates could be attached. Speeds of over 40 kph were not allowed with them.

The vehicle performed well, even under the most difficult conditions in Russia. There were a few broken axles of the rear leading wheels, plus heavy wear on the front-wheel suspension. The troops themselves described the vehicle as especially useful in war.

Parts of the "tracked cycle" formed the basis of the "Springer" medium charge carrier (Sd.Kfz. 304), of which the NSU Works built a total of 50 units from 1944 to the end of the war.

A file note of August 16, 1941, explained that according to Army Weapons Office information, no vehicle of that design type other than the small tracked cycle was available for the time being. A vehicle for seven men with a design like that of the small tracked cycle was being developed, though. At that time there was just one

Above: The small tracked cycle for telephone cable (Sd.Kfz. 2/1). Below: The small tracked cycle for heavy cable (Sd.Kfz. 2/2).

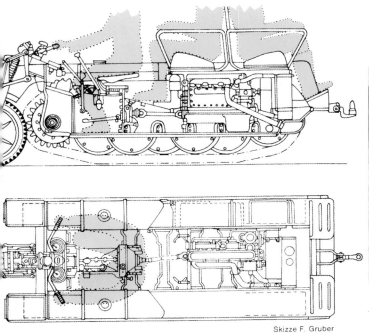

Skizze F. Gruber

Of the large "*Kettenkrad*," Model "HK 102," there exist only these drawings. The vehicle was obviously designed to carry five men.

During the war, attempts were also made to improve the off-road capability of the Volkswagen *Kuebelsitzer* Type 82 by attaching rear tracks. These attempts, designated Type "155," created a number of running-gear types, which did not prove themselves in the end.

test model of the so-called large tracked vehicle. The vehicle was designated "HK. 102." Fitted with a two-liter, 65 HP Stump motor, it had a total weight of 250 kg. The completion of development was not expected in less than two years. The vehicle never went into production.

The Porsche "*Volksschlepper*," Type 113, was also to be a halftrack vehicle. For military use, it could also be used with rear seats. The vehicle was not built.

For the sake of completion, a development of Dr. Ing. h.c. F. Porsche may be noted, which created a halftrack vehicle in 1943 by modifying a VW *Kuebelwagen*. Several prototypes with the type designation "155" were created; in place of the rear wheels, they had tracked running gear supported by truncated-cone springs. Here too, no series production took place.

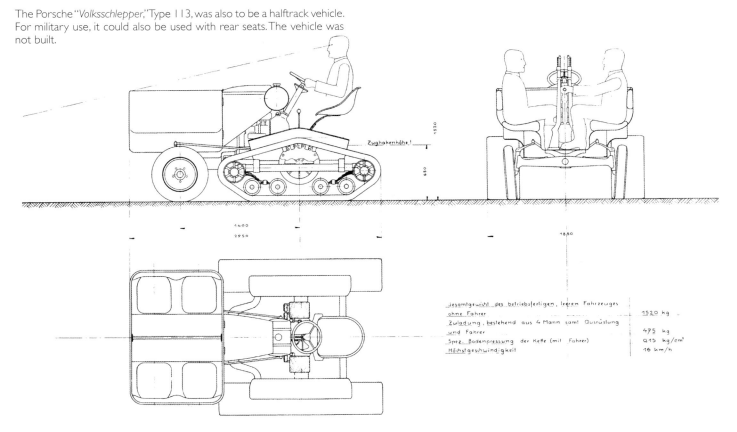

The small UNIC Type "TU I" was also acquired by the German Army in large numbers.

The vehicle was used to supply the armored units of the Austrian Army. The picture shows the prototype in rough terrain.

There was a single example of the Type "AFRS" artillery towing machine.

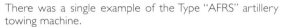

This vehicle, after being taken over by the *Wehrmacht*, was used to tow the light 3.7 cm Pak. Typical of the many rebuildings of French halftrack vehicles is this armored self-propelled mount for the 7.5 cm Pak 40 L/46.

The SOMUA Type "MCL" heavy artillery tractor was captured from the French in 1940. Large numbers of them and the smaller Type "MCG" fell into German hands.

The wheeled/halftracked "ADMK" vehicle developed by Steyr-Daimler-Puch for the Austrian Army is shown in pre-production form, running on wheels.

After the occupation of Austria in 1938, the German forces took over all of the country's military equipment.

Besides individual Citroen-Kegresse and Maffei test vehicles, they found seven "AFR" halftracks made by the Austrian auto factory of AG, which were originally used by armored troops to transport materials of all kinds to supply the tanks, including off the roads. One of the "AFRS" prototypes was set up as an artillery towing vehicle. The vehicles were ordered at the end of 1936 and delivered in 1937. They were used by the German *Wehrmacht*.

In 1940, a great number of usable halftrack vehicles were captured from the French and used by the German *Wehrmacht*. Among others, the "TU 1" light towing wagon (number Zgkw U 305 (f) and "P 107" number Zgkw. U 305 (f)) made by Unic-Georges Richard in Puteau on the Seine, were used to tow light infantry support weapons.

The older "MCG" types made by the SOMUA firm in Saint-Quen (number Zgkw. S 307 (f) and "MCL 6" number Zgkw. S 303 (f)) were also used as artillery towing vehicles. A number of these vehicles were fitted with makeshift armored bodies in 1943-44 and served as self-propelled mounts, armored troop carriers, and supply vehicles.

Wheel/Track Vehicles

The Steyr-Daimler-Puch AG, Austria's largest maker of motor vehicles, had become known for a series of notable special military vehicles. Among others, they had developed the "M 36 off-road-capable 0.6/1-ton towing wagon," which was designated "ADMK." This small towing wagon with air-cooled motor was useful for all tasks in which usual road speeds plus the greatest possible off-road capability were needed. For them, the Type "ADMK" had a wheeled and a tracked running gear. The transition from wheels to tracks was

The same vehicle was used in fully tracked form. Typical of it are the large-diameter road wheels.

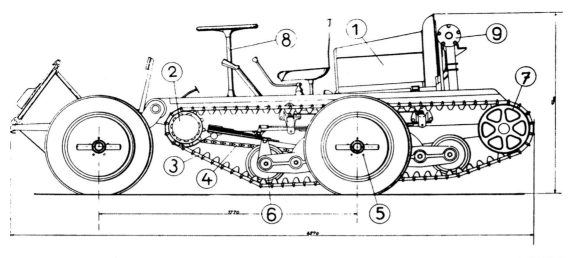

The production vehicle of the "ADMK" type had smaller diameter road wheels. The details of the chassis are easy to see in this drawing.

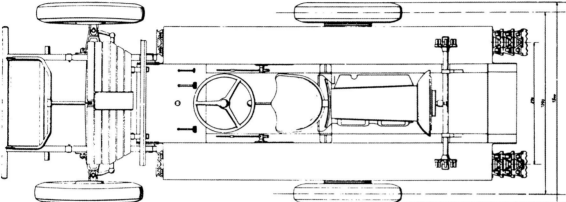

Chasis
1. Motor
2. Drive axle
3. Track
4. Drive track for wheel driving
5. Driven wheel
6. Track carrier roller
7. Track tension roller
8. Steering
9. Wheel holder

3824 MK

3826 MK

3825 MK

The "ADMK" vehicle on wheels and as a halftrack vehicle.

The "ADMK" vehicle is shown as a fully tracked vehicle, with the change of the running gear made by relocating the wheels.

made by removing the wheels, which were fastened by a simple central lock and placed in the wheel holders on the vehicle during travel on tracks.

Four different ways of running were possible with this vehicle:

1. As a wheeled vehicle,
2. As a fully tracked vehicle,
3. As a halftrack vehicle,
4. On wheels in a manner that allowed the tracks to be switched on, in order to cross difficult places on soft ground or in snow with extra help from the tracks.

Low centers of gravity, narrow track widths, and great handiness made these towing wagons well suited for use in the mountains. In the transition from wheeled to tracked running, their handiness was even heightened in that by folding up the front axle attachment, the vehicle's length was shortened by nearly a meter, which particularly made driving through roadless forests easier.

For use in showy or very swampy terrain, the tracks could be widened to 340 mm by added sheet-metal plates.

The "M 36 off-road-capable 0.6/1-ton towing wagon" was planned to carry three men.

A new body for the "ADMK" vehicle was developed by the German *Wehrmacht*, and is seen here as a wheeled and tracked vehicle.

The body of another prototype was changed somewhat, and the headlights were attached to the front of the body. Tests with wider and more show-capable tracks were also made.

As machine-gun carriers, the crew and a heavy machine gun with 6000 rounds and the required equipment could be carried. When towing infantry or mountain guns or grenade launchers on trailers, they carried the crews plus quantities of ammunition weighing up to a maximum of 300 kg. In addition, they could tow a trailer load of up to 1000 kg.

The great towing power of this off-road-capable towing wagon also allowed its use in road- and railroad-building, as well as in airport service. Between 1935 and 1938, 334 of these motor carts were built.

The pre-series vehicles still built by Austro-Daimler in Wiener-Neustadt had road wheels of greater diameter than those of the production model.

During the war, these vehicles were used in northern front areas, but were first fitted with new bodies for this use. The bodies were fully enclosed and fitted with doors, which increased the weight of the ready-to-march vehicle to 1730 kg. The payload was 500 kg. The vehicle was designated "ADMK/WARK." Some of the vehicles were fitted with truck bodies.

In 1937, Steyr-Daimler-Puch created a test model of a somewhat larger wheel/track vehicle of Type "ADAT." The vehicle was in-tended as a light artillery towing machine and had a six-cylinder, 80 HP "M 640" motor installed. The payload was 1600 kg. The vehicle was built during attempts to create a light artillery towing wagon and a light tank chassis. The War Technical Office of the BM f LF had, by Order 78, 200-PV/36, planned an evaluation trial for artillery towing vehicles and invited the firms of Steyr-Daimler-Puch, AG and Saurer, Fiat, and Graef & Stift. The evaluation tests were carried out in January 1937 and clearly showed the superiority of the full-track or halftrack vehicles over those with all-wheel drive as towing wagons for light artillery. On the basis of these results, 160 of the Saurer "RR 7" vehicles to be described later were contracted for. The further tests for a light tank chassis were broken off by the events of March 1938. Since Steyr had originally taken part in the evaluation tests with a four-wheel-drive six-wheel Type "ADGR" vehicle, the "ADAT" type was quickly developed. In fact, though, only one vehicle was built.

On May 31, 1939, the Empowered General for Motor Vehicles issued a contract to the Steyr firm for a light wheel/track vehicle for use by mountain troops to tow light infantry and antitank guns and transport ammunition. The vehicle was also to be used by the airborne troops. With a total weight of 1.6 tons and driven

As an artillery towing machine and the chassis for a light tank, a few of the Type "ADAT" were developed by the Steyr-Daimler-Puch AG. The pictures show this vehicle running on wheels and tracks.

Finally the German *Wehrmacht* ordered the improved Type "M/K," of which only prototypes were built. The vehicle was bigger than its forerunners and fitted with a stronger motor.

Left: The picture shows the "M/K" vehicle being used in snow as a fully tracked vehicle.

The German *Wehrmacht* ordered 140 of these vehicles, which were issued to German army units as "medium armored observation vehicles" (Sd.Kfz. 254).

The unarmored version of the "RR 7" was used as a "repair vehicle" with a payload of 1.5 tons.

by an air-cooled 45 HP four-cylinder motor, wheel speeds of 70 kph were supposed to be attained. The first version of this "light wheeled/tracked vehicle, Type M/K" did not meet the requirements, and a second test model was under construction with a projected delivery date in the spring of 1942. In terms of engine power, fuel consumption, steering, and body formation it represented a further development of the "ADMK" type. It also utilized the experience gained in winter tests on rough snowy and icy terrain. The development was not finished.

A heavier vehicle of this kind was the Type "RR 7" of the Austrian Saurerwerke AG, which was built for the *Wehrmacht* as a "medium armored reconnaissance wagon (Sd.Kfz. 254)." The tests of this vehicle went back to 1935. At that time the Saurer works cre-

ated the Type "RR," a wheeled/tracked wagon on which the change from wheels to tracks could be made even during slow driving. After an evaluation test, fifteen of them were contracted for in January 1937. A subsequent contract called for a single series of 140 units, and their production ended in November 1940. An unarmored version of the vehicle served as a "repair vehicle" with a payload of 1.5 tons. An improved Type "RK 9" was tested in 1940-41. But they were too complicated and were not developed further.

The halftrack towing machines of the German *Wehrmacht* reached a high point in the development of high-value military vehicles. Planned for use in Western Europe and built with typical German thoroughness, they could later amount to only a burden on production and maintenance. Yet they were among the most notable products of the German military motorization.

The Austrian Saurer works were also involved in the planning of the light artillery towing machine; they presented the wheeled/tracked "RR 7."

The final version in the development of the wheeled/tracked vehicles was the prototype of the "RK 9," an armored reconnaissance vehicle, which appeared in 1941-42. It did not go into series production.

C. Armored Halftrack Vehicles 1919-1945

Since the development of armored vehicles was essentially forbidden by the Treaty of Versailles, all efforts at that time were limited at first to basic research on armored fully tracked vehicles. The halftrack was neglected at the time, but the development of wheeled/tracked vehicles was promoted. A basic agreement on the use of armored vehicles in future wars could not be formulated, since nobody could really collect sufficient experience. It remained for military leaders such as Guderian, Fuller, and de Gaulle to create modern ideas.

The development of halftrack vehicles at that time was described by Fritz Heigl as follows: "The unification of tracked running gear and steerable front wheels lessens the speed without increasing off-road capability and the full value of tracked vehicles. The economic advantage of the vehicles in war is in the use of production chassis. Armored vehicles of this type decrease the compelling superiority of pure tracked vehicles off roads and the high speed of armored vehicles on roads."

During later years, these arguments proved not to be so decisive, since additional experience and the use of better materials had of-fered new solutions. Above all, it was the design of special vehicles for the military that created valuable models.

Halftrack vehicles of the new type had a large range of uses where a good network of roads existed. Good on-road performance, sufficient off-road performance, and high towing power could be united satisfactorily in these vehicles. In the French Army in particular, armored and unarmored halftrack vehicles were common. In the army motorization of those days, though, the battle tank was given priority as before. The motorization of other troop units progressed only hesitantly because of the high expenses.

The view of Liddell Hart that "fully motorized fighting forces had to be capable of performance comparable to that of fully mobile Mongolian troops" was accepted emphatically by the creators of the new armored troops. Here again it was the meager German industrial capacity that limited the motorization of the German Army. Using Britain and France as models, at first theoretically and later practically within a limited framework, escort infantry was based on production wheeled vehicles. At this time, for the first time, the promotion of armoring for these vehicles was stressed. The realization of this request took years to be fulfilled.

In 1934, Rheinmetall was already urged to collaborate with Buessing-NAG to create the first version of the "7.5 cm self-propelled mount L/40.8." The picture gives a side view of the vehicle with the cannon in its rotating turret.

The front of the vehicle with the tower in the 9 o'clock position. The front axle is supported by a transverse leaf spring. The rear view shows the good ballistic layout of the armored body and the easy access to the engine compartment.

One of these chassis was fitted with a different type of armored body toward the end of the war and served as a fire-control vehicle for a "V 2" rocket unit. The picture shows the cables attached to the vehicle and used to fire the rockets.

This wooden mockup of the third prototype of the "7.5 cm self-propelled mount" had low bodywork, different running gear, and a new turret layout.

The prototype shows the favorable form of the armored body and the excellent mounting of the primary weapon, which was very outstanding in performance in its time.

The front view of the vehicle emphasizes the low overall structure of this development.

Details of the chassis and the front entry hatches are easy to see in this picture. Buessing-NAG designated this chassis "BN 10 H."

In the meantime, the Army Weapons Office, as already portrayed, had had a series of high-quality halftracks developed, which had been divided into six basic versions and issued to the troops in large numbers. Within the framework of this production, several special developments for armored vehicles had appeared, which now were to be taken up further. By 1934 the Rheinmetall firm, in collaboration with Buessing-NAG, had received a contract to create an armored assault vehicle. Three test versions of this "7.5 cm self-propelled mount L/40.8 (Model 1)" had been built; they varied in terms of firing height, length, and width. The vehicles' bodies had 20 mm side and bow armor, while the roof and bottom were protected by 8 mm of plate. With a four-man crew and a total weight of 6000 kg, the top speed was 60 kph. A 7.5 cm tank gun with an initial velocity of 685 m/sec was installed. The field of elevation went from -9 to +20 degrees, and the turret turned 360 degrees sideways. For the chassis, Buessing-NAG of Berlin-Schoenewalde made three "BN 10 H" (chassis no. 2006-2008) and one "BN 11 V" type (chassis no. 2005) available. Of them, the Type "BN 10 H" was fitted with a rear engine. These chassis were variants of the five-ton towing vehicle that was produced in large series, with Buessing-NAG responsible for their development. The second model of the "7.5 cm self-propelled mount L/40.8" was contracted for in 1936 by the Army high Command. For it, Rheinmetall built two weapons with mounts, while Buessing-NAG again supplied the vehicle and armor. On March 23, 1936, Buessing-NAG accepted the contract for the vehicle designated "Pz. Sfl. III on Chassis m. Zgkw. 5 ton (HKp 902)." Four of these vehicles, fitted with rear engines, were produced (chassis no. 2009-2012). With a total weight of

A vehicle from the final version "HKp 902" was used in North Africa and destroyed there. It was called "armored self-propelled mount III on 5-ton medium towing wagon chassis."

From top to bottom: The "HL kl 3 (H)" chassis planned for use with armored bodies was made by Hansa-Lloyd-Goliath.

In 1935, one of these chassis was fitted with the body of a tank destroyer. In its turret were a 3.7 cm Pak L/70 and two MG 34.

The front view shows the shot-deflecting form of the armored body, the MG 34 in a ball mantlet, plus the MG on the turret roof for anti-aircraft use.

Details of the open-topped turret with the turning ring for the anti-aircraft machine gun.

eleven tons, the armor plate was between 6 and 20 mm thick. The vehicle was driven by a 150 HP Maybach "HL 45" motor; its top speed was 50 kph. Four-man crews were planned. Two of the chassis were fitted with armored bodies and used in Libya during the war. One of the chassis appeared toward the end of the war as an armored fire-control vehicle for V 2 rockets. The Flak 4 Unit requested a similar type, the "Sfl. 5 cm Flak 41," in 1941. The Buessing-NAG type designation for this vehicle was "HKp 903." Only one of these chassis (no. 2013) was built. An off-road-capable halftrack vehicle was requested as a gun carrier with a high road speed. With 6 mm armor, the vehicle had a total weight of 12.5 tons. An eight-man crew was planned. Buessing also produced other prototypes of the "HKp 901," two of which were built (chassis no. 2014-2015).

The normal chassis of the five-ton towing machine were rebuilt into self-propelled tank destroyers on order from the Weapons Office dated August 14, 1941. The Altmaerkische Kettenfabrik created open-topped armored bodies for them. The driver's seat remained unprotected. Nine vehicles of a first makeshift type, with a total weight of 10.5 tons, were built. Fitted with a Russian 7.62 cm Pak and carrying a five-man

crew, some of these vehicles were troop-tested in Libya. They were called "Diana."

In the development of three-ton towing wagons, for which the Hansa-Lloyd-Goliath firm was responsible, rear-engined chassis for armored bodies also appeared from 1935 on. Under contract from the Army High command, Rheinmetall created a "3.7 cm self-propelled mount L/70" for use as a tank destroyer. Using the "HL kl 3 (H)" chassis, there arose a halftrack vehicle with a 3.7 cm gun and two light machine guns. The armor was supported by the frame. The swiveling turret was borne by the gun mount. To fight against air targets, a turning ring with an attachment for the second MG was fitted atop the turret. The 3.7 cm tank gun had an initial velocity of 900 m/sec, an elevation field from -7 to +20 degrees, and a traverse of 360 degrees. The total weight of the vehicle was 6000 kg. It was not assigned to the troops; only one test model was built.

An improved version of the chassis appeared in 1936 as Type "HI kl 4 (H)." It had a six-cylinder motor in the rear and was planned for a total weight of 6500 kg. The staggered running gear and greased tracks had one more road wheel than the towing-machine types. A five-man crew was planned. The external dimensions of the chassis were 5200 x 2000 x 1090 mm. The armor was 20 mm thick in front and 11 mm on the sides. The end of the development of these rear-engined armored halftrack vehicles came with the Type "H 8 (H)" made by Hanomag. This vehicle, built in 1938, originally used

a six-cylinder, 120 HP Maybach "HL 49 TRWS" motor, which was later replaced by the 115 HP "HL 54." A Variorex gearbox was used, and the total weight was eight tons; only prototypes were built.

Many varieties of armor appeared on halftrack towing machines during the war. Those used as self-propelled mounts in particular were fitted with armor plate to protect vital parts and drivers' compartments. Armored versions were even used to tow Army Flak guns, but the types with armored bodies had considerably reduced payloads, as the vehicles were developed mainly as towing machines and not as load carriers. This disadvantage was especially clear in the so-called armored vehicles that served as the basis of the later armored troop carriers. In the "Maultier" development too, which turned production 3- and 4.5-ton trucks into halftracks, there were also armored versions. Three hundred Opel trucks were fitted with light armor and armed with the 15 cm Foglayer 43 with 360-degree swiveling. The vehicles known as "15 cm *Panzerwerfer* 43 (Sd.Kfz. 4/1)" were officially introduced in May 1944. Their fighting weight was 7.1 tons. With a three-man crew and 20 rounds of ammunition, they carried 8 mm armor. Another 300 of these vehicles were ordered as ammunition carriers by September 1943.

Also of note is the development of very simplified towing machines, done at Hitler's urging. The resulting light and heavy *Wehrmachtsschlepper* were planned with armor protection for their motors and cabs from the start. Only the heavy version included

In 1938 the Type "H 8 (H)," the last of the three-ton towing machines in the HK 600 series, was built by Hanomag. Only a few prototypes were made.

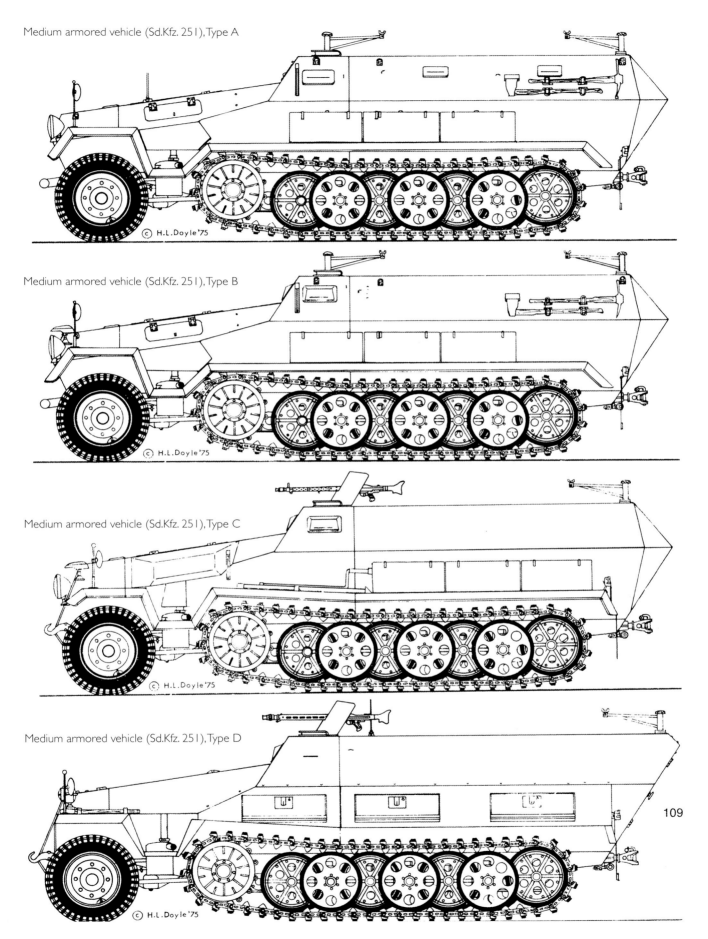

Medium armored vehicle (Sd.Kfz. 251), Type A

© H.L.Doyle '75

Medium armored vehicle (Sd.Kfz. 251), Type B

© H.L.Doyle '75

Medium armored vehicle (Sd.Kfz. 251), Type C

© H.L.Doyle '75

Medium armored vehicle (Sd.Kfz. 251), Type D

109

© H.L.Doyle '75

an unarmored towing wagon. In the eight-ton towing class, an order from the Weapons Office on August 14, 1941, resulted in a tank destroyer with a 360-degree traverse for use in Libya. This vehicle was designated "7.62 cm Pak 36 on 8-ton Zgkw (Artemis)." The four-man crew was protected by shellproof armor. The design was finished and a model was made. In 1944, several of the eight-ton towing machines with armored bodies were rebuilt as fire-control vehicles for V 2 rocket units.

For the heaviest version of the halftrack towing machines, the 18-ton type made by FAMO, an armored self-propelled mount was created to carry the 8.8 cm Flak 37. Originally, 112 of them were contracted for in 1942. The Weserhuette in Bad Oeynhausen actually delivered fourteen of them in 1943.

Senior General Heinz Guderian expressed himself on the motorization of the armored escort infantry in his book, *Memories of a Soldier*: "The development of the tracked vehicles for the complementary weapons to the tanks never picked up the speed that we wanted. It was clear that the results of the tanks had to be all the greater, the better the riflemen, the artillery and the other weapons of the divisions could follow them directly on the march. Thus we advocated halftrack vehicles with light armor for the riflemen, the engineers, the medical corps, armored self-propelled mounts for the artillery and the antitank units."

From this advocacy there arose, with the designation "medium armored vehicle" (Sd.Kfz. 251), a lightly armored version of the three-ton towing wagon. The Hanomag firm in Hannover was responsible for developing the chassis, and they created the "H kl 6" type as a variant of the "H kl 6." Buessing-NAG of Berlin-Oberschoeneweide developed the armor-plated body in cooperation with the Deutsche Werke in Kiel.

The preliminary work began in 1937. In 1938 a contract, numbered VIII b/211-2003/38 (G IV b-113/38), was given for a 0 series. For the first time, the designation "medium armored personnel transport wagon" (MTW) appeared. It was meant to be used by the fast troops and the motorized troops. The first unit to receive such vehicles, in the spring of 1939, was a company of an infantry regiment of the First Armored Division.

The armored body of the medium armored personnel transport was mounted on a chassis like that of the three-ton light towing wagon, on which, as opposed to the normal structure, several changes to the radiator, steering wheel, fuel tank, and exhaust system had been made.

The armored body consisted of bow, middle, rear, side, and bottom armor. The main parts were made of shotproof plates welded or riveted together, and mounted at an angle to the main shot direction and secure from horizontal SmK shots. The body was attached to the chassis by connecting pieces.

The bow and middle armor covered the engine and driver's areas. The lower front plate of the bow armor protected the steering arms and shock absorbers.

The middle and rear armor formed the fighting compartment, which was separated from the engine compartment by a bulkhead. The rear armor consisted of two parts. The side and bottom armor protected important parts of the chassis.

The fighting compartment was open at the top. There was a two-piece door in the rear wall. At the front of the compartment, by the armor plate over the driver, a removable and swinging armor shield was attached, in which a machine gun was mounted. Over the transverse bar at the rear end of the compartment was a swinging arm that held another machine gun.

For protection against dust and rain, the fighting compartment could be covered by a canvas canopy mounted on four insertable rods.

The driver's and radioman's seats were adjustable. In Type C, the floor could be removed along with the seats in order to adjust the steering brakes easily.

At eye level there were adjustable flaps in front of the driver and radioman, plus adjustable visors to the left and right, with their sight slits protected by changeable glass pieces. On the long sides were four seat boxes or benches, under which ammunition or baggage could be stored.

The most numerous armored vehicle in the German *Wehrmacht* was the medium armored troop carrier (Sd.Kfz. 251), of which there were four basic versions, which are shown here:

Type A: recognized by the two visor openings on the rear body sides.

Type B: the side visors are gone, with only one visor opening planned by the co-driver.

Type C: the front bumper is gone, the bow plate is different, and the side openings to the engine room are newly designed.

Type D: only straight plates are used. The side visor flaps are gone. The rear now juts out at the top.

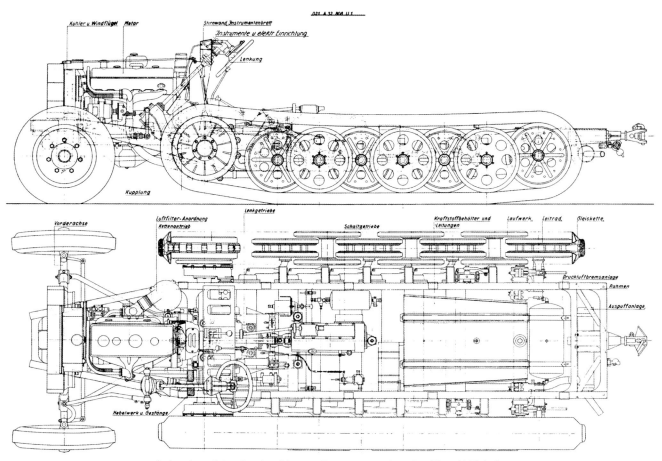

A drawing of the chassis of the medium personnel carrier (Type H kl 6 p).
The front view of the chassis.

The seats of Type C were adjustable in height for traveling and war marching.

Type A had two visors in the upper sidewalls of the rear armor; they were protected by replaceable glass panels. Type B differed externally only in lacking these side visors that Type A had.

The armor plate in the general shot direction was 4.5 mm, with 8 mm on the sides and rear.

By mid-1940, three versions of this vehicle reached the troops, with Types A and B differing essentially from Type C as follows:

Hanomag and Hansa-Lloyd-Goliath had begun the series production of the chassis in 1938. While 190-18 tires were normally used, chassis 796-1 to 796030 (Hanomag) and to number 320285 (Hansa-Lloyd) had extra 7.25-20 tires for use. The group vehicles were basically fitted with just one battery, while radio and other special versions had two batteries. The fuel tank had to be changed accordingly. In the tropical version of the vehicle, the wind deflector for engine cooling was changed and an improved air filter was used.

	Types A & B	Type C
OUTSIDE		
Bumper	present	none
Cool air flaps	present	none (water temperature regulated by adjustable radiator cover)
Trenching tools & signal flags	attached to armor walls	attached to fenders
Rear license number	on number plates	painted on rear plate, making access to track tightener easier
INSIDE		
Equipment holder Fasteners	on welded bars or screws	on screwed-on brackets
Driver's seats	bucket seats	new uniform tank seats
Inside lights	searchlights	hand light with 5-meter cable
MP 38 holder and magazine pocket	not present, later attachment possible	Holder for two MP 38 & magazine pocket
Seat benches	not adjustable, no back	Seats adjustable for travel and march, with back and head brace.
Gun holders	6 for 6 rifles	2 racks for 4 rifles each
Fire extinguisher Attachment	outside on right	inside on left door
Visor flaps	straight adjusting lever	bent adjusting lever

Between September 1, 1939, and March 31, 1940, a number of armored troop transport wagons were assigned anew to the armored divisions. Borgward, among others, produced chassis no. 320831 to 32039 in 1940, 32040 to 322450 in 1941, and 322451 to 323081 in 1942. On April 28, 1941, the Army high command called for the OKH ChiefH.Ruest. to upgrade light armored vehicles to the SS special level. The OKH Wi Rue office, though, did not agree to the desired result of this upgrading. The overloading and tension in similar SS production, such as of heavy tanks, would be so strong already that the upgrading of lightly armored vehicles to the SS level would somehow be disadvantageous for the production of heavy tanks or the most urgently needed naval and *Luftwaffe* production. The meaning of the production of lightly armored vehicles was nevertheless recognized to its full extent, and the OHK Chief H Ruest was requested to eliminate the difficulties of the primary and secondary producers when possible. This support worked out so that a series of additional firms were brought into the production program. The assembly of the vehicles was assigned to the firms of Weserhuette in Bad Oeynhausen, Wumag in Goerlitz, and F. Schichau AG in Elbing. The chassis were built by Adler in Frankfurt, Auto-Union in Chemnitz, Hanomag in Hannover, and Skoda in Pilsen. In 1942, the firms of Stoewer in Stettin and Maschinenfabrik Niedersachsen (MNH) in Hannover were also involved. The armored bodies were supplied by Ferrum of Laurahuette, Schoeller & Bleckmann of Muerzzuschlag, Bohemia of Boehmisch-Leipa, and Steinmueller in Gummersbach. The raw material needed per vehicle amounted to 6076 kg unalloyed and alloyed iron, and the price per vehicle was RM 2,560.

Immediately after the union with Austria, some 30 million Reichsmark were made available by the *Wehrmacht* for important war production. Another 10.5 million for the building of an armor-plate factory in Kapfenberg were assigned to the Boehler firm, while Schoeller-Bleckmann in Muerzzuschlag received 2.91 million for the same purpose. In 1938-39, Boehler had already delivered 140 bodies for armored observation vehicles (Sd.Kfz. 254), and until 1941 they built not only the armored ammunition transport wagon (Sd.Kfz. 252), but also 250 bodies for the armored observation vehicle (Sd.Kfz. 253). In 1942-43 they produced 1075 bodies for the light troop transporter (Sd.JKfz. 250). As of the summer of 1940, the production of armored bodies took place in the new factory at Kapfenberg.

Schoeller-Bleckmann moved body production to Muerzzuschlag in 1940, and from 1940 to 1944 they produced 232 bodies for the medium troop transporter (Sd.Kfz. 251).

At the beginning of 1940, delays in body production occurred at Schoeller & Bleckmann due to a shortage of molybdenum. The supply situation and the differences of competence within individual service arms are typified by an excerpt from a letter sent by the Chief of Army Supplying to the Reich minister of the Interior on May 17, 1941: "Through your letter of April 9, 1941, you informed my Army Weapons Office that you have advised the Steyr Works positively to carry out the production of 24 armored road vehicles for the *Waffen*-SS quickly, in equal urgency with all other production. It is not at all about vehicles for the *Waffen*-SS and thus the establishment of combat troops, but about vehicles that are to serve purely police functions behind the front. Even more important is the erroneous assumption that the delaying of sixty bodies for light armored personnel carriers for Army supplying in favor of the armoring of police vehicles behind the front, via immediate communication with the Boehler firm, would be bearable. The armored personnel carriers for the equipping of the combat troops are lacking to a degree that only my military colleagues, involved with the daily supply problems, can judge. The armored personnel carriers are intended for rifle brigades and engineers in the armored divisions. The urgent insistence for the Afrika-Korps could not yet be fulfilled if a single issuing of 30 units to the Luftwaffe were necessary."

In 1940, a total of 348 medium armored personnel carriers (SPW) were produced. In 1941 there were 947. Although the vehicle in its final form could only count as a transport vehicle, the growing use and the arming of the individual variants during the last war years resulted in a combat vehicle of limited utility. The tank had finally found its classic partner. The entire production for 1942 numbered 1190 units. In October 1942, Hitler considered the suggested installation of foglayers on the three-ton armored towing machine to be very important. At first, twenty of these vehicles were to be delivered per month.

The Type D appeared in somewhat simplified form in 1943, after being raised to the SS class. Only straight armor plates were used, and the rear was strikingly redesigned. The side visor flaps were dropped and replaced by slits. The year's production for 1943 numbered 4250 vehicles; in 1944 the number rose to 7800 units. The vehicles remained in production until the war ended. In 1944, Guderian emphatically requested that the three-ton armored grenadier

wagon remain in large-series production without any changes. The needs of the armored engineers and intelligence troops also had to be met with this vehicle. The outstanding but very complicated tracks of these vehicles formed a constant maintenance problem. There were cast track links (Type Zgw. 50/280/140 or Zgw. 5001/280/140), or a pressed version (Type Zpw. 5001/280/140). While the first number indicates the type of track, the second shows the track width and the third the track division. On February 24, 1944, the Ch H Ruest u. BdE announced that instead of the formerly used tracks with rubber pads for towing wagons, tracks with steel caps, called

Light trailer sleds based on Russian models were towed by medium armored troop transporters. This towing wagon is a Type A (with visor flaps on the rear side walls).

Left: Type D, introduced in 1943, had a simplified armored box with only straight plates. The pictures show front and rear views of the vehicle during training.

From top to bottom: The Type C vehicle, side view, MG mounted in armor shield, and anti-aircraft swinging arm and lashed down.

The driver's compartment of the medium armored troop carrier.

Stahllaufketten, would gradually be issued. Thus the top speed on roads would be limited to 30 kph. There would also be an increased danger of skidding on roads. Off the road, the steel tracks were equal to those with rubber pads. The Army Technical V. Blatt of June 1, 1944, stated: "The medium armored troop carriers were tested with tracks whose rubber pads were replaced by steel caps. The latter have not proved themselves in troop testing. The steel caps loosen easily and are often lost. The steel caps are therefore replaced again by rubber pads (W 112g)."

It is now appropriate to look at the variety of versions that made this type of vehicle become not only the most versatile, but also the most numerous armored vehicle of the German *Wehrmacht*.

As already noted, the medium armored vehicle (Sd.Kfz. 251) was the basic vehicle for all other versions. As Sd.Kfz. 251/1, the medium armored troop carrier appeared in two forms. It was used either for a group with two light machine guns or for two heavy machine-gun crews. The first version carried 12 men, while the second had 11. The total weight was about nine tons. Using Sd.Kfz. 251 0r 251/1, the firm of J. Gast KG in Berlin-Lichtenberg created a version that carried the Heavy Launching Frame 40. The angle setting was made by hand. Fin-stabilized 28 cm explosive or 32 cm flame grenades were fired. Fog charges were also available. The maximum shot value was 1.8 km. Vehicles of Types A through D were used for this.

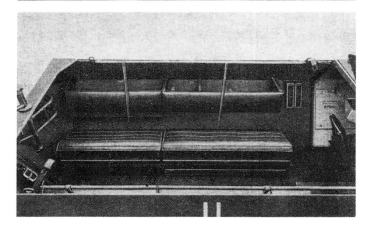

The left and right sides inside the body, with ground holders.

Sd.Kfz. 251/1 (Type C), side and front views, with a look into the driver's compartment. The front motor plate, now made in one piece unlike those of Types A and B, is easy to see. There were two versions of this vehicle (left).

The vehicle in action with the Heavy Launching Frame 40. The warheads were easy to follow in flight (below).

The Heavy Launching Frame 40 was mounted on all types of the medium SPW since 1940. The pictures show the setting of the launching direction on both sides of the vehicle.

The vehicle with loaded launching frames; the angle setting for the range had to be set by hand.

The Medium Armored Radio Wagon (Sd.Kfz. 251/3), Type C, with details of the radio devices it carried.

Antenne für Fu 8

Antenne für Funksprechgerät f

5

The Gaubschat firm of Berlin received a contract on September 1, 1940, for installations on Sd.Kfz. 251 for armored observation batteries. Troop testing was to begin in the spring of 1942. The Sd.Kfz. 251/2 was planned for a heavy grenade-launcher troop and had a fighting weight of 8.64 tons. An 8 cm heavy launcher was installed for firing from the vehicle; 66 rounds of ammunition were carried. The eight-man crew could also use the weapon outside the vehicle. The grenade launcher's baseplate for use outside the

Sonder Kfz 251/3 Special Vehicle 251/3

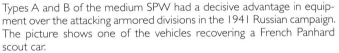

Sd.Kfz. 251/2 as a medium armored troop carrier (grenade launcher). The picture shows the 8 cm heavy launcher mounted on a baseplate.

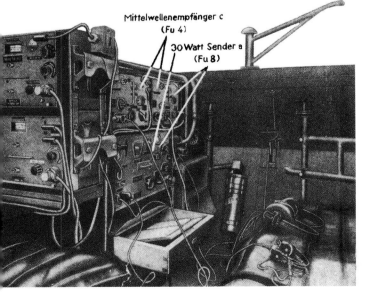

Mittelwellenempfänger c (Fu 4)

30 Watt Sender a (Fu 8)

Types A and B of the medium SPW had a decisive advantage in equipment over the attacking armored divisions in the 1941 Russian campaign. The picture shows one of the vehicles recovering a French Panhard scout car.

vehicle was attached to the front plate of the motor. The medium armored radio wagon (Sd.Kfz. 251/2) came in no fewer than nine different variations. It basically carried a seven-man crew, and its fighting weight was some 8.5 tons. The following radio device combinations determined its combat value: I = Fu. 8, Fu. 5 and Fu. Spr.f; II = Fu. 8, Fu. 4 and Fu.Spr.f; III = Fu. 8, Fu. 5 and Fu.Spr. f; IV = Fu. 7, Fu. 1 and Fu.Spr.f; V = Kdo.Fu.Tr.Fu. 11 and Fu. 12; VI = Fu.Tr.100 Mw(gp); VII = Fu.Tr.80 Mw(gp); VIII = Fu.Tr.30 Mw(gp); and IX = Fu.Tr.15 Kzw.(gp). One MG 34 or 42 with 2010 rounds of ammunition were carried.

The medium armored troop carrier (IG)(Sd.Kfz. 251/4) could hold a light IG crew and 120 rounds of 7.5 cm ammunition. The fighting weight was 7.74 tons. The infantry gun was coupled to the vehicle. A second version of this vehicle was used exclusively as an ammunition carrier. These vehicles were no longer built after 1943.

Also dropped as of 1943 was the medium armored engineer wagon (Sd.Kfz, 251/5). It ran as Group Wagon 1, 2, 3, or 4 in the motorized engineer platoons, carrying a nine-man crew and two machine guns. The radio equipment varied according to use. The medium armored command vehicle (Sd.Kfz, 251/6) had an eight-man crew and a fighting weight of 8.5 tons. One Fu. 12 and one Fu. 19 were installed. The medium armored engineer wagon (Sd.Kfz. 251/7) appeared in two versions, and was used as either a Group Wagon 1, 3, and 5 or 2, 4, and 6 within the platoon on the armored vehicles of the light motorized engineer companies. Seven- or eight-man crews and engineer equipment were carried. Sometimes assault bridges to cross large trenches were carried on the outer sides of the vehicles. There were two versions of the medium armored ambulance (Sd. Kfz. 251/8), differing only in their radio equipment. Two-man crews were planned, and the entire weight was 7.47 tons.

Senior General Heinz Guderian is seen in his armored command vehicle (Sd.Kfz. 251/6) during the 1940 French campaign. His vehicle is one of the first Type As.

From top to bottom (at left): An Sd.Kfz. 251/6 with changed antenna attachment, seen during the 1940 French campaign.

The medium armored command wagon (Sd.Kfz. 251/6) Type B shows details of antenna attachment in the first action in Russia.

An aircraft command vehicle (armored command wagon) of Type B in action in North Africa.

The Sd.Kfz. 251/7 carried, among other things, quick bridges for crossing terrain hindrances on both sides of the body.

The medium armored engineer wagon (Sd.Kfz. 251/7) also appeared in two forms. A heavy 2.8 cm *Panzerbuechse* 41 is hung on the vehicle.

Type A vehicles were later rebuilt as medium armed ambulances (Sd. Kfz. 251/8). This picture shows one of them in North Africa.

Type C vehicles were also used for this purpose. These vehicles basically had no armament.

The medium armored troop carrier (7.5 cm K 51 L/24)(Sd.Kfz. 251/9) served as a support vehicle in armored grenadier units. The pictures show the Type C vehicle from the front and side.

A gun wagon of Type D, which was especially numerous.

A contract from the Weapons Office to the Buessing-NAG firm on March 31, 1942, called for a medium SPW with 7.5 cm L/24 tank gun. The firing height was 1710 mm, and a three-man crew and 32 rounds of ammunition were to be carried. The medium SPW (7.5 cm K 51 L/24) (Sd.Kfz. 251/9) weighed 8.8 tons. As of June 1942, two test models were troop-tested in Russia. A first series of 150 units went into production in June 1942.

On December 2, 1942, it was decided that the 75 available 7.5 cm StuK L/24 should be used to arm grenadier wagons and available 8-wheeled armored scout cars. In addition, a new series of this gun was preferred to arm grenadier wagons. It should first be attempted not to commit any capacity of the Pak 38 to the new run of the 7.5 cm tank gun, thus the further building of the 5 cm KwK L/60 could be halted at once.

Late Type D vehicles were given extra armor protection for the guns, and also along the sides. Toward the end of the war, these

support vehicles appeared in ever-greater numbers. In 1940 the platoon leaders' wagons had 3.7 cm Pak guns installed. The armor for this weapon consisted of either the Pak gun's original shield or a somewhat lower wraparound type. With a fighting weight of 8.01 tons, these medium armored troop carriers (3.7 cm Pak) (Sd. Kfz. 251/10) carried a six-man crew. They also carried a Heavy *Panzerbuechse* 39 with 40 rounds of ammunition. Their production was halted in 1943. The contract for the medium armored telephone wagon was issued on January 16, 1942. It was used by the large motorized telephone troops. This Sd.Kfz. 251/11 came in two more versions, as vehicles for the medium field cable troop 10 (gp) and the light field cable troop 6 (gp). Up to five-man crews were carried. The first vehicle of this type was delivered on August 15, 1942. Later the measuring troops were also equipped with the medium armored measuring-equipment wagon (Sd.Kfz. 251/12), which carried most of the equipment. The artillery of the armored

In the final version, the side armor for the main armament was drawn far back, so as to protect the crew better.

While one crewman cleans the gun, others replace the vehicle's damaged road wheels.

Originally, the platoon leaders' vehicles were armed with the 3.7 cm Pak behind the original shield (Sd.Kfz. 251/10). The pictures above show side and rear views of the Type A vehicle.

Later the original armor shield was replaced by a lower version. The picture above shows a Type C version of this vehicle.

At right, the platoon leader's vehicle is seen in action in Russia. In both cases, the vehicle is a Type C.

units received the following three special vehicles: the medium armored sound-receiving wagon (Sd.Kfz. 251/13), the medium armored sound evaluating wagon (Sd.Kfz. 251/14), and the medium armored light evaluating wagon (Sd.Kfz. 251/15). They did the same jobs as the earlier unarmored versions on three-axle truck chassis. The 8.62-ton medium armored flame wagon (Sd.Kfz. 251/16) was next on the list. Attached to the sides of the armored body were two flamethrowers behind armor shields. The nozzles had 14 mm diameters. A 7 mm hand flamethrower and an MG 42 were also carried. The crew numbered three men. The Sd.Kfz. 251/17, the medium armored troop carrier (2 cm), came in three versions. The first one used the unchanged armor body, in the middle of which a 2 cm Flak 38 was installed. Because of the narrow opening of the fighting compartment, the traversing field was limited. The vehicle carried 600 rounds of ammunition. The narrow fighting compartment was eliminated in the *Luftwaffe* Fla version, as the body was not only widened, but also made so that the side armor walls folded outward. Thus, not only was a 360-degree traverse achieved, but the crew had sufficient freedom of movement. Up to eleven men were needed to operate it. The last version had an unprotected fighting compartment that could be widened sufficiently by folding down the side plates. The motor and driver's cab were protected as usual. The medium armored observation wagon (Sd. Kfz. 125/18) was already contracted for in 1940, and finally appeared in 1943 to replace the light version. The medium armored telephone truck (Sd.Kfz. 251/19) was used by the telephone operation troops. In 1942 a heat-sensing device, equipped with a 60 cm receiving mirror and a bolometer, had already been discussed in a work discussion of the OKH WaF. As of 1944, a number of these infrared devices were ready for use at the front. Above all, they were used by the armored

The medium armored telephone vehicle (Sd.Kfz. 251/11).

Armored flame wagon, Type D, in action (Sd.Kfz. 251/16).

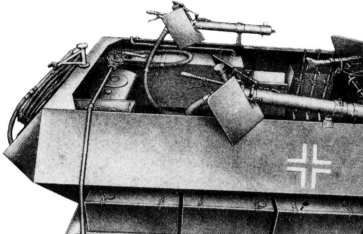

From top to bottom: The medium armored flame wagon (Sd.Kfz. 251/16): rear view of a Type C.

The body of the armored flame wagon shows the flame pipes mounted on the sides and the containers for the flaming liquid.

An armored flame wagon Type D with its crew wearing protective masks. An MG 42 is mounted on the front armor shield.

After a 2 cm Flak 38 had been mounted inside the crew's space of the medium armored troop transport (2 cm) (Sd.Kfz. 261/17), the second version used a mounting of the weapon similar to that of the one-ton towing machine. The front of the Type C was protected by armor plate, while the shooting platform at the rear had only a shield to protect the gun.

troops as night driving and night targeting devices. Medium SPWs were fitted with this equipment for battlefield lighting (Sd.Kfz. 251/20). A "Panther" unit was equipped with it toward the end of the year as a test. The camouflage designation for the project was "Uhu." The aerial superiority of the Allies, which was growing ever stronger, required the use of armored anti-aircraft vehicles as a countermeasure.

In order to increase the defensive power of the armored grenadiers, anti-aircraft armored troop carriers (Sd.Kfz. 251/21) were put into service in 1944, carrying either triple 1.5 cm or 2 cm AA guns. The 1.5 cm Fla MG 151/15 was usually used. Its traverse field was 360 degrees.

At right, a medium SPW with a 60 cm Flak spotlight for invisible (infrared) battlefield lighting (Sd.Kfz. 251/20). Disguised as "Uhu," some of these vehicles were assigned to "Panther" units in 1945 for testing; some of them showed considerable success.

In the special Luftwaffe version, the body was modified, with the sidewalls being made to fold out. The picture at far left shows the unit equipped with them, with the command vehicle in the foreground. A frame antenna is attached (previous page).

Here a Type C command vehicle with folding side walls is shown, plus a frame antenna and an MG 34 behind a shield (previous page, lower left).

The combat vehicles themselves show the installation of the 2 cm Flak 38 on a vehicle in normal condition (previous page and below).

Medium SPW with triple MG 151/15 or 151/20 as an anti-aircraft vehicle of the armored grenadier units (Sd.Kfz. 251/21). Almost all of these vehicles saw service only toward the end of the war, and suffered from the usual supply difficulties.

At Hitler's personal order, the 7.5 cm Pak 40 (L/46) was mounted on the medium SPW (Sd/Kfz. 251/2) at the end of 1944. Hitler judged this to be one of the best efforts of the war.

In Armored Division 45, there were three of them with the armored reconnaissance unit and three in each company of the armored grenadier battalion (gp). In many cases, the armor of the weapons was strengthened or modified in the field. The last item on the SPW list was Sd. Kfz. 251/22. The Army's Technical V. Blatt No. 82 of 1944 said of it: "The medium SPW 251/2 (7.5 cm Pak 40) has no turret, but carries the Antitank Gun 40 behind a shield." The whole upper mount with the barrel and shield of the 7.5 cm wheeled Pak 40 was set unchanged on a pivot in the middle of the fighting compartment of the SPW. On November 27, 1944, Hitler ordered that the SPW planned for equipping with the 7.5 cm gun not be held back until December, but be delivered in November armed with the 7.5 cm Pak 40. Further, all thus equipped vehicles were to go to all divisions as model vehicles, so as to prepare for the rearming of available SPW. On November 29, 1944, Hitler stressed again that he placed decisive value on an immediate series production of the Pak 40 on the 3-ton SPW. On December 12, 1944, Hitler called the SPW with the Pak 40 one of the best developments of the war. He emphasized again the urgency of immediate conversion, and indi-

cated again the necessity of having all wheeled Pak 40 be given the small cutouts necessary for mounting them on armor shields.

The assigning of these armed SPW within Armored Division 45 gave nine vehicles to the antitank unit and three to the armored reconnaissance unit. Six more went to the cannon platoon of each battalion. The vehicles were overloaded by the installation of these guns.

For Armored Division 45, there were 90 SPW planed: 30 Sd.Kfz. 251/1, 24 Sd.Kfz. 251/3, six Sp.Kfz. 251/16, 12 Sd.Kfz. 251/21, and 18 Sd.Kfz. 251/2. Because of the war's events, the number of variations had to be limited sharply.

Because of the large numbers of these vehicles, there were numerous variants that were made by the troops themselves. It is needles to go into them closely; but one prototype is worthy of mention, since it was introduced officially according to the *Führer's* order in 1943. At that time, making the heavy 8.8 cm wheeled Pak gun mobile was vital in the judgment of the Army command. Although the chassis was overloaded by it, the 8.8 cm Pak 43 L/71 was installed experimentally on the medium SPW. Except for the engine cover all the armor was removed, and the crew was protected only by the gun shield. Field use never took place.

One Type A vehicle was used as the basis of a makeshift self-propelled mount for an 8.8 cm Pak 43 L/71. The rear-armored body was removed, and the gun was placed behind an armor shield. The pictures show it being shown to Hitler in 1943.

The Czech firms, especially Skoda in Pilsen and Bohemia in Boehmisch-Leipa, continued production after the war. After the unchanged Sd.Kfz. 251 had been built, substantive changes were made in the course of further development. The armor box was changed and closed at the top, and the complex running gear, particularly the tracks, became simplified. Finally, a Tatra Diesel engine was installed. The vehicle runs to this day as "OT 810" in the Czech People's Army.

At the beginning of SPW development, not only a group vehicle, but also a half-group type, was requested. For this the chassis of the one-ton towing machine developed by the Demag firm was available.

A Type D medium SPW towing a 7.5 cm Pak 40.

At the end of 1944, an armored command vehicle of Type D is seen with firing spotlight and shear telescope.

For years after the war ended, Czechoslovakia built the medium SPW for their forces. The picture shows Type "OT 810," which had a different motor from the German version, ungreased tracks, and a fighting compartment with a closed roof.

The following differences from the "D 7" towing machine existed:

- Armored hull instead of steel-plate hull,
- shortened running gear,
- modified radiator, steering wheel, fuel tank, and exhaust system.

The firm that developed the Type "D 7 p" chassis was DEMAG of Wetter, in the Ruhr, while Buessing-NAG in Berlin-Oberschoeneweide continued to build the armored body. The first prototypes, which appeared in 1939, were sometimes still powered by the Maybach "NL 38" motor, but the production models made as of 1940 used the Maybach "HL 42 TUKRR" motor. A dry two-plate clutch of Mecano PF 20 K type was attached to the motor. From there the power flowed through a cross driveshaft to the transmission. A semi-automatic Maybach shift-regulating gearbox of Type "VG 102 128 H" was installed. The individual speeds were selected in advance by a small hand lever, and the shifting itself was done by a low-pressure system after the clutch was used. The gearbox had seven forward and three reverse speeds. From the gearbox, the steering drives were driven by a pair of cone wheels. Steering with the steering wheel activated only the front wheels at first. The whole steering system worked like a normal equalizing drive. Under greater pressure, the steering brakes were applied. From the steering drives on, the drive wheels at the front of the tracked running gear were driven by a crown-wheel system. The drive wheels carried the twelve turnable drive-wheel rollers that meshed with the tracks. The running circles of the drive wheels were fitted with rubber segments. The brake drums for the hydraulic brakes were located in the drive wheels.

The road wheels were mounted on cranks and sprung by torsion bars that were set between the transverse carriers. They overlapped each other, and were arranged alternately for inside and outside carrying. They were formed as changeable sheet-steel disc wheels with rubber tires. Drive wheels, inner road wheels, and leading wheels moved the drive teeth of the tracks laterally. The hubs of all road and leading wheels ran on roller bearings.

Each of the two tracks Type "Zpw 51/240/160" consisted of 38 links connected by bolts. The drive teeth of the track links were formed as grease cups with closing screws. Each link bore a rubber pad held by four screws. The front axle was formed as a swinging fist axle and supported against the hull apex by a leaf spring. The tube axle was mounted on a triangular brace in the middle of the hull and braced to receive the pushing power.

To dampen the vehicle's swinging, the front axle was fitted with two hydraulic shock absorbers.

The steering power was transmitted from the hand wheel through a worm gear to a steering-column lever and a double cam. The cams activated the hydraulic brake cylinder of the steering brakes. The hull was made of sheet steel with riveted-in transverse members. The main member, from which the steering drive was suspended, was formed as a tube axle and screwed to the hull accordingly. The 140-liter fuel tank was installed at the rear of the vehicle. A sprung trailer hitch was attached to the rear of the hull; its coupling hooks on either side were movable and could turn 360 degrees.

The bow armor, bow shield, and stern armor formed the armored body. The bow and stern armor were screwed together. They consisted of shotproof armor plates welded together and set at an angle to the main shot direction, and could withstand horizontal SmK fire. The body was screwed to the armored hull of the chassis. The bow armor, with the removable armor shield, covered the engine compartment. The shield protected the steering rods and shock absorbers. The rear armor formed the fighting compartment, which was separated from the engine compartment by a bulkhead. The fighting compartment was open at the top. In the rear wall of the body was an entry door boltable from inside. The fighting compartment could be covered with a panel resting on three insertable rods. The backs of the driver's and passenger's seats could be

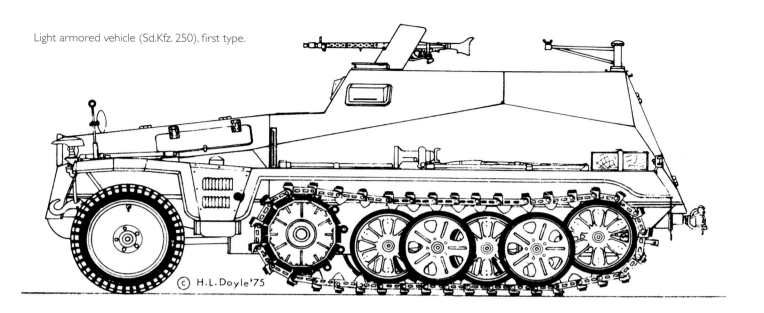

Light armored vehicle (Sd.Kfz. 250), first type.

© H.L.Doyle '75

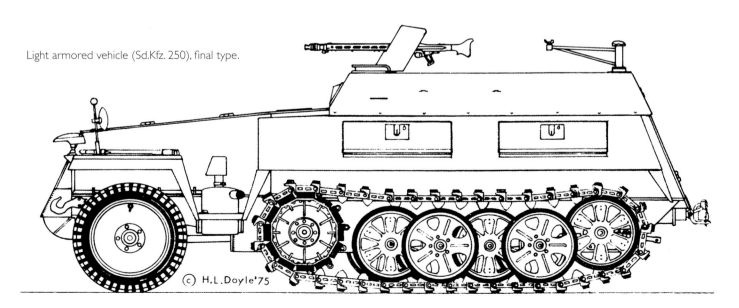

Light armored vehicle (Sd.Kfz. 250), final type.

© H.L.Doyle '75

The left side of the light SPW (Sd.Kfz. 250): h = large cable shear; f = tow-line; d = starter crank; b = jack with crank, rod, and block; g = spade; and e = crowbar.

h **f** **d** **b** **g** **e** **b**

The right side of the light SPW: l = axe; k = pick-axe.

i **k**

The right side with opened equipment compartments: i.l = fire extinguisher in box; i l = axe in box; and a = three tool brackets.

i, l **i₁** **a**

folded down, and were also adjustable to face the driving direction. At eye level before the driver and passenger were adjustable visor flaps, with their vision slits protected by replaceable glass protectors. To the driver's left was an adjustable visor flap, to the passenger's right a visor.

The armor was 14.5 mm thick in front, and 8 mm on the sides and back. The vehicle's total weight was 5.8 tons. A crew of up to seven men could be carried. The first bodies were made by the Deutsche Edelstahlwerke AG in Hannover-linden and L & C Steinmueller in Gummersbach.

During the war, the Evens & Pistor firm in Helsa, Thuringia, was made exclusively responsible for assembling these vehicles. In 1942 the firms of Weserhuette of Bad Oeynhausen,

Front and rear views of the vehicle.

The driver's compartment: o = two 70 × 270 × 54 protective glasses; s = hand light; t = holder for shielded headlight when not in use; p = two protective glasses, 70 × 150 × 54; q = signaling flagstaff; n = two long and one short safety windows in box by passenger's seat; u = first aid kit inside door; and rl = fire extinguisher on left rear sidewall.

Right sidewall: p = two protective glasses, 70 × 150 × 54.

Wumag of Goerlitz, Wegmann of Kassel, Ritscher of Hamburg, and Deutsche Werke of Kiel were included in this production program. Chassis came from the Demag Works in Wetter/Ruhr and Mechanische Werke in Cottbus. The armor was made by the Bismarckhuette in Upper Silesia. Boehler of Kapfenberg produced 1075 bodies for these vehicles in 1942-43. The raw material needs per vehicle included 4563 kg of alloyed and unalloyed iron, and the price per vehicle was RM 20,240. The vehicle's official designation was "light armored vehicle" (Sd.Kfz. 250). It was the basic vehicle for all light armored troop carriers. Until 1941, no reliable production figures are available; in 1942, 1340 of these vehicles were built. As with the medium vehicle, a basic modification took place in 1943, now using flat armor plates. In that year, 2900 light SPW of all versions were built. The production was halted in 1944, after another 1690 units had been built. The Phillip Schiffswerft Ebert & Sons in Neckarsteinach produced some of the bodies at that time.

The numerous variations will now be described individually: There were two versions of the light SPW (Sd.Kfz. 250/1); the first type carried a light machine-gun crew with two MG 34. One gun was mounted in the armor shield and the other on the right sidewall of the body. The platoon leaders' vehicles had only one MG 34 as armament.

The second version of Sd.Kfz. 250/1 served as a means of transport for a heavy machine-gun crew and carried not only the MG 34 in the armor shield, but also a second one on the right sidewall. The MG Mount 34 was carried in an attachment on the outside of the vehicle. The fighting weight was 5380 kg.

In January 1940, a contract for a compressed-air launcher (Device 170) on a light SPW was issued. It fired 10.5 cm shells weighing some 6 kg at a range of about 1000 meters. The launcher was developed by the Skoda Works. Demag supplied the "D 7 p" chassis with compressor setup. The vehicle's total weight was 5.5 tons. One unit was built, and a further development was initiated, having a larger compressor that was supposed to increase the shot range to 1800 meters. The light telephone armored wagon (Sd.

The light SPW built from 1943 on was fitted with a very simplified body without recording a change in its versions. The pictures show this improved vehicle, which stayed in production until 1944.

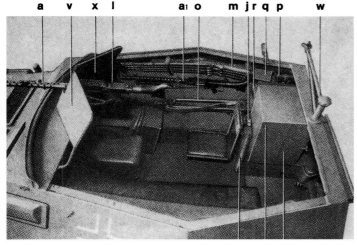

a   v   x   l   a₁ o   m j r q p   w

i   c f,d

b u   e g m,b₁,h,j₁,w c   q s a t

f,d,c₁ p j i r l

e   g   y,i,h,j₁,n   s u   a

w   t   b

The left inside of Sd.Kfz. 250/1 for two heavy MG crews: b = MG Mount 34; u = AA swinging arm; e = MG belt drum carrier; g = Cartridge Sack 34; m, b1, h, j1, w = clothing cabinets, mount equipment, Barrel Holder 34, Barrel Protector 34, hand angle scope and shear scope in external box; c = cartridge box under seat bench; q = canopy window; s = Gas Mask 34; a = MG 34 in armor shield; t = armor shield; l = 4 rifles; r = canopy post; i = barrel holder; j = barrel protector; p = canopy; f, d, c1 = Cartridge Sack 34, Belt Drum 34 and Bullet Case 34 in ammunition cabinet.

Pictures from top down: Sd. Kfz. 250/1 for a group with two light machine guns: a = MG 34 in armor shield; v = armor shield; x = radio; l = MP 38, a1 = MG 34 on right wall; o = tripod for MG 34; m = 4 rifles; j = Barrel Protector 34 with contents; r = canopy; q = flare and signal ammunition in container; p = flare pistol; w = AA swinging arm; l = Barrel holder 34; c = Bullet Case 34 in ammunition cabinet; f, d = cartridge sack in ammunition cabinet, plus Belt Drum Carrier 34.

v   k a₁ u n,o   b

The left inside of Sd.Kfz. 250/1: e = Belt Drum Carrier 34; g = Cartridge Sack 34; y, l, h, j1, n = hand angle scope and shear scope, Barrel holder 34, Barrel Protector 34 and clothing bags in outside baggage box; s = canopy window; =u = Gas Mask 34; a = MG 34 in armor shield; b = Cartridge Case 34 under seat bench; t = canopy post; and w = AA swinging arm.

Sd. Kfz. 250/1 for two heavy MG crews: v = radio set; k = magazine carrier for MP 38; a1 = heavy MG 34; u = AA swinging arm; n, o = flare pistol, flare and signal ammunition; and b = MG Mount 34 on attachment outside on vehicle.

u   o   a   s   q k j b i   p

l f c₁,e,g,t

Pictures from top down: the right inside of the light telephone armored vehicle (Sd.Kfz. 250/2): u = driver's seat; o = armor shield; a = MG 34; a = telephone set for "small telephone troop (mot)"; q = 4 rifles; k = canopy; j = flare and signal ammunition; b = Cartridge Case 34 in cabinet; i = flare pistol; p = AA swinging arm; l = canopy window; f = MP 38 with ammunition; c l, e, g, t = Belt Drum Carrier 34, Barrel Protector 34, clothing bags, hand shear scope and angle scope in outside box.

The left inside of Sd.Kfz. 250/2: m = canopy post; c = Belt Drum Carrier 34; d = Cartridge Sack 34; s = telephone equipment; o = armor shield; n = Gas Mask 34; a = MG 34 in armor shield; l = canopy window; q = 4 rifles; k = canopy; and b = Cartridge Case 34 in cabinet.

m   c d   c₁,e,g,t s   o h   a

p

b k q   s   l

View of the left inside, rear space with winch drum and equipment box (Sd. Kfz. 250/2): c = Belt Drum Carrier 34; s = telephone equipment; n = Gas Mask 34; o = armor shield; a = MG 34; and s = more telephone equipment in outside box.

Front part of the interior of Sd.Kfz. 250/3, light radio armored vehicle: l = Gas Mask 34; a = MG 34 in armor shield; j = MP 38; r = radio set, depending on use; e, m, s = Barrel Protector 34, clothing bags, hand shear and angle scopes in baggage box.

c   s   n o a

l   a

s   s

e, m, s   r

Pictures from top down: View inside Sd.Kfz. 250/2 showing the telephone cable containers attached to the front fenders.

The right inside of Sd.Kfz. 250/3: l = 3 rifles; q = radio equipment, depending on use; g = flare and signal ammunition; and f = flare pistol.

The left inside of Sd.Kfz. 250/3: d = Cartridge Sack 34; c = Belt Drum Carrier 34; p = canopy window; c1, k, b = Belt Drum Carrier 34, box for five fog cartridges, Cartridge Case 34 under seat bench; n = canopy; and o = canopy post.

For command tasks, Sd.Kfz. 250/3 was equipped with long-range radio equipment, and thus also fitted with the box antennas used on radio vehicles. A vehicle thus equipped served as a means of transport for Field Marshal Rommel in North Africa (below and top of next page).

The 1943 version of the light radio armored wagon (Sd.Kfz. 250/3).

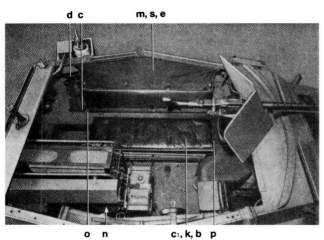

a

s

a g k″ j₁ i₁ b n c e h p. p₁   o d,t,y,z l s

a

u₃   y   n₂

w   x   o   k   n₁

j   v   i₂   u

i   j   g g x w n₁ n₃ o k i i₂

y   c n₂

Pictures from top down, opposite page: Side view of the light observation armored vehicle (Sd.Kfz. 250/5): a = MG 34 in armor shield, s = AA swinging arm on rear covering plate.

Lower left: The inside view of Sd.Kfz. 250/5: w = 3 signal flags; x = Standard 40 with cap holder for azimuth circle; o = box for Azimuth Circle 40 with contents; K = field canteen; n1 = shear scope after use of scope brace; z1 = hand shear scope, here housed behind radio set; u = canopy window; i2 = Gas Mask 34; v = canopy post; and l = 2 gas masks.

Right center:
The right inside of Sd.Kfz. 250/5: a = MG 34; g = ammunition for MP 38; k1 = three field canteens; j1 = cooking utensils; i1 = Gas Mask 34; b = Cartridge Case 34; n = case with shear scope; c = Belt Drum Carrier 34; e = Barrel Protector 34; h = 6 hand grenades; p1 = radio sets, depending on use; m = flare and signal ammunition; d, t, y, z = Cartridge Sack 34, canopy, clothing bags, hand shear and angle scopes behind the radio stand; s = AA swinging arm; q = part of radio equipment; n2 = lashing for telescope brace.

Lower right:
The left inside of Sd.Kfz. 250/5: l = gas mask; j = cooking utensils; g = MP 38 with ammunition; x = Standard 40 with cap holder for azimuth circle; w = 3 signal flags; n1 = shear scope brace; n3 = lashing for scope brace; o = box for Azimuth Circle 40; k = field canteen; l = gas masks; i2 = lashing; c = Belt Drum Carrier 34; y = clothing bags.

Kfz. 250/2) had a four-man crew. It carried the Light Field Cable Troop 6 (gp). There were five versions of the light radio armored wagon (Sd.Kfz. 250/3). The following combinations of radio sets were possible: I = Fu. 7 and Fu. 1 8; II = 8, Fu. 5 and Fu. Spr.f; III = Fu. 8, Fu. 4 and Fu. Spr.f; IV = Fu. 8 and Fu. Spr.f; and V = Fu. 12 and Fu. Spr.f. With a four-man crew, the fighting weight was about 5.34 tons. There are contradictory official data on the Sd.Kfz. 250/4. According to D 600, Page 270a of July 6, 1943, this number was reserved for the light anti-aircraft armored wagon. According to Army Tech. V. Page 1944 no. 82, it was the light observation armored wagon. With the armored artillery observation wagon on "D 7 p" chassis, there were production difficulties in March 1940, since it was a new design. Obviously, the troop anti-aircraft vehicle was not introduced. The light observation armored wagon, which later appeared as Sd.Kfz. 250/5, had a four-man crew and an Fu.Spr.f radio. Later versions had an Fu. 8 SE 30 set and an Fu. 4 set. The Army technical page cited above lists the Sd.Kfz. 250/3 as a light reconnaissance armored vehicle. The light reconnaissance vehicle replaced the earlier Sd.Kfz. 253 as of 1943. In 1942, the AHA/In 6 directed Buessing-NAG to develop a light SPW with a heavy launching device. The contract was issued in March 1942 and a development specimen was finished, but the vehicle did not go into production.

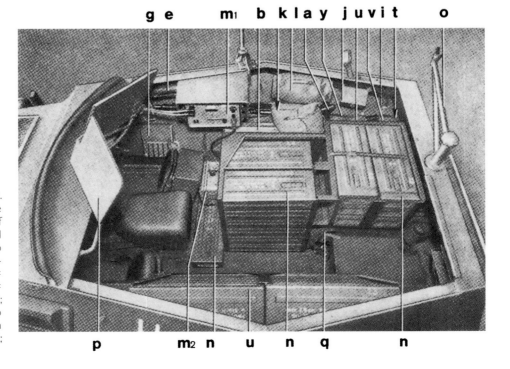

The light ammunition armored wagon (Sd.Kfz. 250/6), Type A, for supplying assault guns with the 7.5 cm Assault Cannon short; the right inside of the vehicle: g = ammunition for MP 38; e = Barrel Protector 34; m1 = radio set, depending on use; b = Cartridge Case 34; k = uniform light; l = clothing bags; a = MG 34 (stowed during march), y = clothing bags; j = flare and signal ammunition; u = field canteens; v = cooking utensils; l = flare pistol; t = hand shear and angle scopes in packing case; o = AA swinging arm; n = 70 rounds of ammunition in 35 cartridge cases; q = canopy; m2 = radio set; p = armor shield.

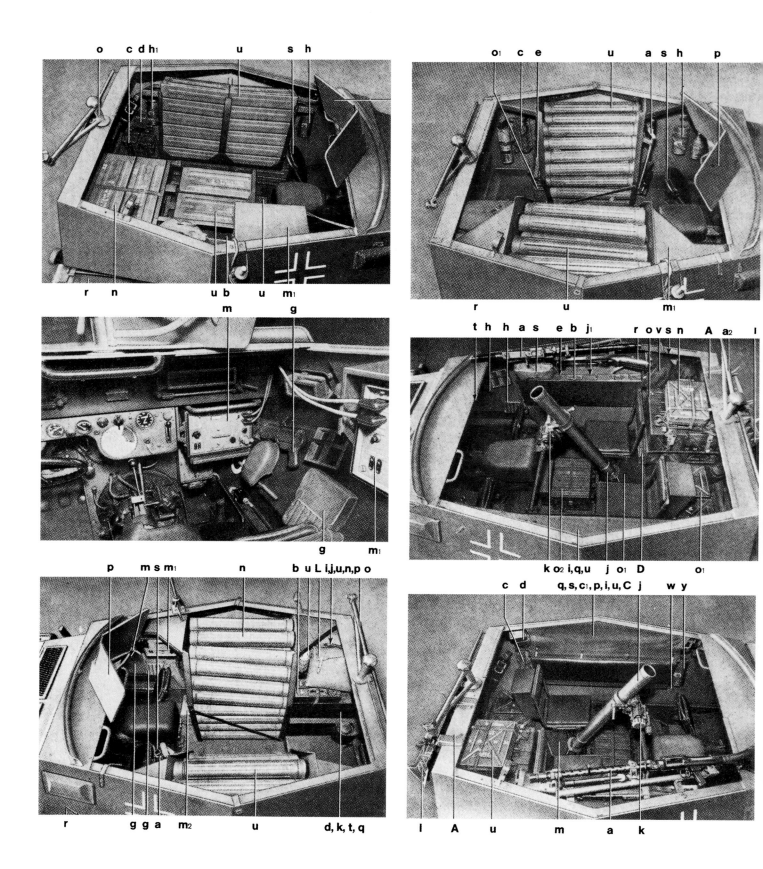

Picture series from top down: Left, the inside of Type A, Sd.Kfz. 250/6: o = AA swinging arm; c = Belt Drum Carrier 34; d = Cartridge Sack 34; h l = gas mask; n = 70 rounds of 7.5 cm ammunition in 35 shell cases; s = canopy window; p = armor shield; m l = radio set; b = Cartridge Case 34; r = canopy post (upper left).

Inside view of Sd.Kfz. 250/6: m, m l = radio sets; g = MP 38 with ammunition (left center).

The light ammunition armored wagon (Sd.Kfz. 250/6) Type B for supplying assault guns with the 7.5 cm Assault Gun 40: the right inside of the vehicle: p = armor shield; m = radio set; s = canopy window; n = 60 rounds of 7.5 cm ammunition in shell racks; b = Cartridge Case 34; v = two cooking pots; l = clothing bags; i, j = flare pistols with ammunition; u, w = field canteens, protective window; o = AA swinging arm; d, k, t, q = Cartridge Sack 34, uniform light, hand angle and shear scopes, canopy; a = MG 34 (stowed); g = MP 38 with ammunition (lower left).

The left inside of Sd.Kfz. 250/6 Type B: c = Belt Drum Carrier 34; e = Barrel Protector 34; n = 7.5 cm ammunition; a = MG 34 (stowed); s = canopy window; h = gas mask; p = armor shield; ml = radio sets; r = canopy post in equipment box on right fender (upper right).

Sd.Kfz. 250/7 for a heavy grenade-launcher troop, right inside: t = radio set; h = ammunition for MP 38; a = MG 34 (stowed); s = clothing bags; e = Barrel Protector 34; b = Cartridge Case 34; j l = barrel with breech; r = 3 rifles; o = 21 ammunition cases; v = canopy; n = ammunition cases with carriers; A = attachments for baseplate (outside on vehicle); D = cartridge case for oil and equipment for grenade launcher; m = special baseplate on bottom of vehicle; j = barrel of grenade launcher; k = dipod (right center).

The left inside of Sd.Kfz. 250/7: c = belt drum carrier; d = Cartridge Sack 34; w = canopy post; and y = gas mask (lower right).

There were two versions of the light ammunition armored vehicle Sd.Kfz. 250/6, which replaced Sd.Kfz. 252 as of 1943. Type A carried a supply of 70 rounds of ammunition for the short 7.5 cm Stuk L/24, while Type B delivered 60 rounds for the long 7.5 cm Stuk L/48. Type A weighed 5.94 tons, Type B 6.09 tons. They carried two-man crews. There were also two versions of the light SPW (s GrW) (Sd/Kfz. 250/7). While one type carried the 8 cm grenade launcher and a five-man crew, the other, as an ammunition wagon, carried 66 rounds of grenade-launcher ammunition. The ammunition wagons also carried a range finder. The "cannon wagon" or light SPW (7.5 cm) (Sd.Kfz. 250/8) served as a support vehicle, and was equipped with the 7.5 cm K 51 L/24. The firing height was 1860 mm. Twenty rounds of ammunition could be carried. The fighting weight was 6.3 tons. The gun shield was 14.5 mm thick in front and 10 mm on the sides. Three-man crews were planned. The Army Tech. V. Page 1943 no. 466 mentioned the introduction of Sd.Kfz. 250/8 on November 10, 1943. Assigning the vehicles was done through the Army High Command In 6. Requirements of the troops were to be made known. The armored reconnaissance units of the armored divisions had been neglected because of the shortage of vehicles. The otherwise useful wheeled vehicles had mostly broken down in Russia. Full-track reconnaissance vehicles were available only in limited numbers. In 1943 Guderian advocated high-performance ground reconnaissance, for which sufficient numbers of one-ton light armored grenadier wagons were needed.

The Weapons Office gave the Gustav Appel firm the job of equipping the light SPW with the 2 cm Socket Mount 38 of Sd.Kfz. 222. In July 1942, three test models were being tested on the eastern front.

A first series of 30 vehicles was already being built at that time. On the basis of a contract issued to the Appel firm by the Weapons Office in March 1942, though, it was fitted with the 2 cm Hanging Mount 38. This mount served to hold a 2 cm KwK 38 and an MG

a
A
I

a₁ t   h   s   a   s   b   e, B r   v z₂ u z₁ s   a₂ A

o₂   P, c₁, C m   D

c d u   q, p, c₁, z₁, i   s   z   c   y w

o₂   a   x

The light SPW (7.5 cm)(Sd.Kfz. 250/8) was the heavy support vehicle of the armored grenadiers.

The pictures from the top down on the left side: Outside view of Sd.Kfz. 250/7, with a look at the baseplate and carrying setup.

The right and left inside of the Sd.Kfz. 250/7 ammunition carrier: B = hand shear and angle scopes in packing cases; z_1 and z_2 = flare pistol and ammunition; u = uniform light; x = canopy window.

Opposite, center: The left and right outside views of the light SPW (2 cm)(Sd.Kfz. 250/9): g = steel wire cable; g_1 = oil canister; U = filling funnel; a = lubrication can; y = muzzle cap; v = 2 cm KwK 38 on socket mount; h = steel wire cable; l = cross pickaxe; d = covers for cannon and MG; k = fuse for explosives; J = radio equipment; x = equipment box for 2 cm gun; c_1 = climbing spurs; y = hand light; q = equipment box for iron rations; z = cleaning gear for gun; f = 4 explosives; a = starter crank; m = fuel canister; and j = entry doors.

Opposite, lower: Vehicle with 1943 armored body and Hanging Mount 38.

b   U,a₁ y   v   u   l   d

k   J   v y x

j   m h   a   f z   q   c₁,y

42, which were linked together. The Hanging Mount 38 was also used on other special vehicles (Sd.Kfz. 140/1 and 234/1). The two weapons could be fired together or separately. Ground and air targets could be fired on. For firing on ground targets, a Turret Aiming Scope 3a (TFZ 3a) was on hand. Over the optics was a device for crude viewing, composed of a back sight, sighting rod, and circular front sight. With external measurements of 1850 x 1500 x 1250 mm, the weight of the mount without the weapons was 540 kg. The elevation range went from -4 to +70 degrees; the traverse was 360 degrees. From above, the mount was protected by a grid attached to the shield and foldable to right and left. The two parts of the grid had bows that folded to the rear, and could be bolted in either position to cover the fighting compartment completely with a canvas sheet. At the back of the mount two seat-holding tubes, which held the height-adjustable seats, were welded on. Radio equipment and antenna were attached to the shield.

A hundred rounds of KwK ammunition could be carried. With a three-man crew, the "light SPW (2 cm) (Sd.Kfz. 250/9)" had a fighting weight of 5.9 tons. The vehicles remained in troop use until the war ended.

Command vehicles also carried the 3.7 cm Pak. As a light SPW (3.7 cm Pak) (Sd.Kfz. 250/10) it had a four-man crew and a fighting weight of 5.67 tons. The traverse was limited to +/- 30 degrees, while the elevation ranged from +25 to -8 degrees. 216 rounds were carried for the 3.7 cm Pak. For a time, the light SPW (Sd.Kfz. 250/11) was also used. With a six-man crew and a 5.53-ton fighting weight, it bore the Heavy *Panzerbuechse* 41 with a firing height of 1875 mm. The vehicle carried 168 rounds of ammunition. At the end of the official type list was, until 1943, the Light Measuring Troop Armored Wagon (Sd. Kfz. 250/12). Three- to five-man crews were planned.

Pictures from top down: Light SPW (3.7 cm Pak) (Sd.Kfz. 250/10); view of the vehicle.

The right and left inside of Sd.Kfz. 250/10: h = 2 MP 38; b2 = 6 ammunition baskets; p = cover for Pak; g = driver's rifle; I = canopy; e = flare and signal ammunition; c = cabinet with cleaning device; d = flare pistol; b1 = 2 ammunition baskets; b = 2 ammunition baskets; f = hand angle scope; o = hand shear scope; j = clothing bags; a = 3.7 cm Pak; k = radio set; n = canopy window; and m = canopy post (left center and below).

The inside of Sd.Kfz. 250/10: I = Gas Mask 34.

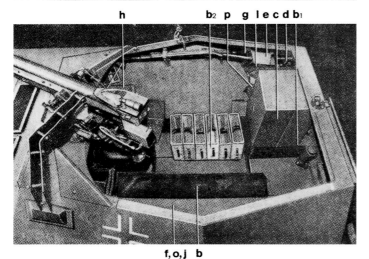

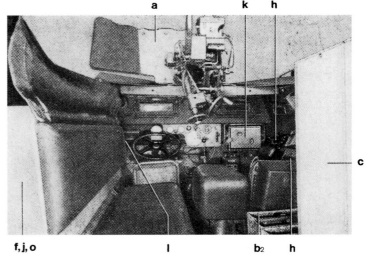

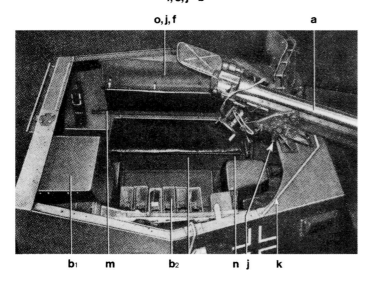

Below: An Sd.Kfz. 250/11 with heavy *Panzerbuechse* 41 of the "Grossdeutschland" Division.

A view of the light field mount outside on the rear (above).

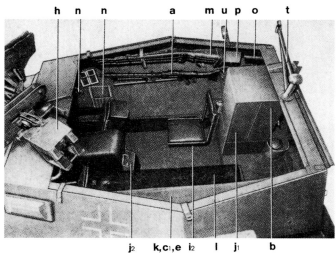

The right outside of Sd.Kfz. 250/11: l = light field mount for heavy *Panzerbuechse*; u = canopy; h = Heavy *Panzerbuechse* 41; and l1 = spur fir field mount (upper left).

The right and left inside of Sd.Kfz. 250/11: n = 2 MP 38; a = MG 34; m = rifles; p = flare and signal ammunition; o = flare pistol; t = AA swinging arm; b = Cartridge Case 34; l, i1, i2 = total of 15 cartridge cases for sPzBu; e = Barrel Protector 34; c = belt drum carrier; k = cover for gun; d = Cartridge Case 34; x = Gas Mask 34; j = cleaning device for gun; q = uniform light; r = clothing bags; y = hand shear and angle scopes; s = radio set; and v = canopy window (left).

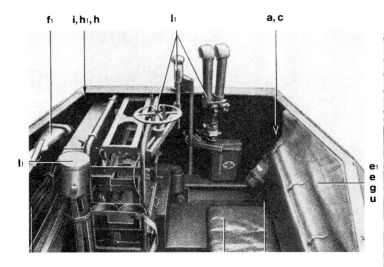

Other than the production varieties, troops often rebuilt vehicles to meet given needs. The picture shows a vehicle of the last type with a 5 cm Pak 38 installed. This vehicle is still on display in Yugoslavia.

Left, from the top down: The light measuring troop armored wagon (Sd.Kfz. 250/12); the rear and bow of the vehicle. The third picture shows the right inside of the armored vehicle: I1 = special equipment for light measuring wagon; f1 = 4 rifles; I = canopy; h, h1 = flare and signal ammunition with flare pistol; d = Shell Sack 34; c, c1 = Belt Drum Carrier 34; e = Barrel Protector 34; g = clothing bags; n = hand shear and angle scopes (in packing case); k = canopy post; b = Cartridge Case 34; a = MG 34; I = Gas Mask 34; f = MP 38 and ammunition; m1 = armor shield; and j = canopy window.

The Sd.Kfz. 10 and Sd.Kfz. 253, which used the same chassis, in action in France in 1940. They served as support vehicles for the heavy units of an armored division with Sf-15 cm sIG on Panzer 1 chassis.

For troop training, here the NCO School in Sternberg, Eats Sudetenland, light armored grenadier wagons equipped with wood-gas systems were used. The vehicles were used for driving-school purposes.

For the assault gun units newly formed in 1940, two types of the light SPW were developed to take on command and supply tasks. These four-side views of the lightly armored ammunition transport wagon (Sd.Kfz. 252) show the unchanged chassis and the closed-top body of the vehicle.

As an observation vehicle of the assault gun units, the light armored observation vehicle (Sd.Kfz. 253) was also available. This vehicle also had a closed top. With it, the series of variants on the basis of the light SPW ended.

Special equipment and an Fu. 8 SE 30 radio set were installed. In the process of making all possible antitank weapons toward the end of the war, individual versions of the light SPW appeared with the upper mount of the 5 cm wheeled Pak.

For the assault-gun units to be set up from 1939 on, armored supply vehicles were required. Using the Demag "D 7 p" chassis, the Waggonfabrik Wegmann in Kassel developed two different armored bodies. The first type was planned as an ammunition carrier, and was used to supply the assault-gun units on the battlefield. These light armored ammunition transporters (Sd.Kfz. 252) normally pulled a single-axle ammunition trailer (Sd.Ah. 32). The total weight was 5.73 tons. The armor was planned to be 18 mm thick in front, and 8 mm on the sides and rear. The series was delivered on October 6,

1941. Also intended for service with assault-gun units was the light armored observation vehicle (Sd.Kfz. 253). Weighing the same, it carried a four-man crew. A ten-watt radio Transmitter h, 2 UKW Receiver h, and one portable Radio Set h were carried. Both special vehicles had closed-top bodies.

Light German-made SPW also appeared in the Czech People's Army after the war ended. Successor models to the light and medium SPW were considered as early as 1939. To replace the 3-ton halftrack series, Hanomag and Demag suggested the "HK 600" series. The type "HK. 601" was seen as a replacement for the 1-ton towing wagon. To replace the light SPW "D 7 p" and medium SPW "H kl 6 p," Type "HKp 602" was considered, of which 3 plus 9 vehicles were contracted for in 1943. The total weight was some 7.5 tons, and

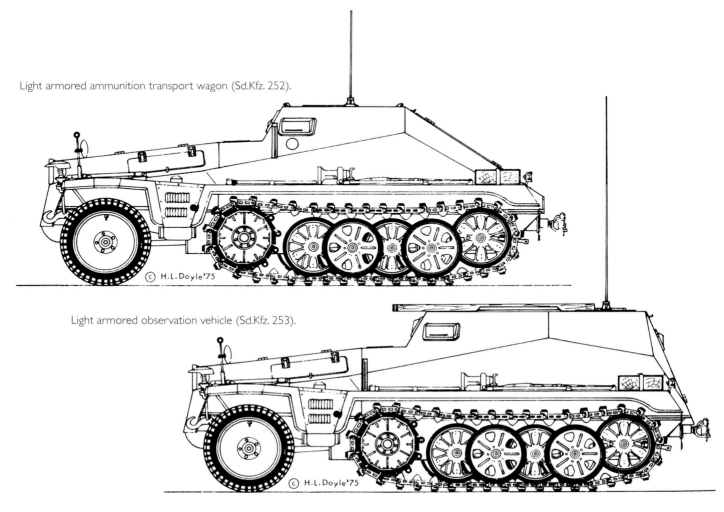

Light armored ammunition transport wagon (Sd.Kfz. 252).

Light armored observation vehicle (Sd.Kfz. 253).

The last of the HKp 600 series was the Demag prototype represented by this vehicle. The type designation was "HKp 606." The pictures show the vehicle from the front and side.

Within the 3-ton halftrack and HK. 600 series was the prototype "HKp 603" created by Hanomag in 1941.

In 1941 came the partly armored Type "HK. 605" developed by Demag; in 1942 it was continued by Hanomag as "Project HKp 607."

From parts of the "Raupenschlepper Ost," the Kloeckner-Humboldt-Deutz AG built the "Type RS 1500 Forest Tractor" of the 9314-16 series right after the war ended. This is one of the last halftracks.

the Maybach "HL 45" engine was seen as its powerplant. The front armor was to be 14 cm thick. Twelve-man crews were proposed. Hanomag was also developing the Type "HKp 603" and built it as a prototype; it was an improved version of Type "H kl 6 p." The six-cylinder, 120 HP Maybach "HL 45 Z" was again installed. The total weight was eight tons. A partly armored version of the Demag Type "HK. 605" was built in 1941-42; it was to weigh 6.8 tons overall. A Maybach OLVAR gearbox and Argus disc brakes were to be used. At the same time, Hanomag developed a somewhat heavier vehicle, designated "HKp 607." Its fighting weight was 9.5 tons. Both vehicles were to use the 170 HP Maybach "HL 50" motor.

Finally, the Demag works at Wetter, in the Ruhr, developed the SPW Type "HKp. 606" as a prototype to replace all earlier SPW types. Modern vehicle components such as automatic transmission and disc brakes were again to be installed. The total weight was some seven tons. The "HL 50" motor gave the vehicle a top speed of 70 kph.

Guderian's request to keep building only the medium SPW (Sd. Kfz. 251) in large series without changes was far-seeing and correct. It allowed a somewhat sufficient supplying of the troops with armored escort vehicles. Even though the original version must be seen as a makeshift solution, the German Army, for the first time, had armored, off-road-capable vehicles available for its infantry within the armored divisions. The technical disadvantages in terms of the vehicle's complexity, its insufficient off-road capability compared to tanks, and its vulnerability to being fired on were largely overcome by progressive action principles. As a final solution, though, a fully armored, full-track vehicle was wanted as a full-value escort for tanks. Such ventures were begun with Panzer 38(t) components toward the end of the war.

Technical Data

Vehicle	Benz-Braeuer Limber	Marienwagen II	Track Machine
Type	Kg	ALZ 13	MSZ 201
Maker	Benz & Cie.	Daimler	J. A. Maffei AG
Years built	1918	1918-1919	1930-1931
Data source	Daimler archives	Daimler archives	Maffei drawing ZM 16334
Motor type	Benz S 125	Daimler La 1264	Magirus V 100
Cylinders	4 in-line	4 in-line	4 in-line
Bore x stroke mm	125 x 150	120 x 160	100 x 150
Displacement cc	7362	7240	4712
Compression ratio	4 : 1	4 : 1	5.38 : 1
RPM	1100	100 [?]	1600
Horsepower	45	50	57
Valves	standing	dropped	standing
Crankshaft bearings	3	3	3 journal
Carburetor	1 Zenith	1 Daimler piston	1 Orkan U 40
Firing order	1-3-4-2	1-3-4-2	1-2-4-3
Starter	by hand	by hand	Bosch BLG 1.2/12
Generator	---	Bosch	Bosch RK 100/12-700
Batteries	---	1 6-volt	1 12-volt 60 Ah
Fuel feed	low-pressure	low-pressure	gravity
Cooling	water	water	water
Clutch	wet multiplate	conical	dry multiplate
Gearbox	pre-selector	pre-selector	Maybach fast
Speeds fwd/rev.	4/1	4/1	5/1
Drive wheels	rear	rear	rear
Axle ratio	1 : 8.87		
Top speed kph	30	10	51.7 w/ fast gear
Range km			
Front axle	rigid	rigid	rigid
Steering	worm gear	screw spindle	screw spindle
Turning circle m	12.8		
Springs front/rear	semi-elliptical, Longitudinal, outrigger	semi-elliptical, longitudinal, screw	semi-elliptical longitudinal
Chassis lubrication	individual	individual	high-pressure
Brake system			
Manufacturer	Benz & Cie	Daimler	Bosch-Dewandre
Effect	mechanical	mechanical	suction
Footbrake works on	gearbox = outer drum	gearbox = outer drum	rear wheels
Handbrake works on	rear wheels,	drive, inner drum	rear wheels
Inner drum			
Wheel type	wooden spoked	cast steel spoked	sheet steel disc
Tires front/rear	1100x120/1200x130	front diam 860 mm 32 x 6/x 2	
Track front/rear mm	1550/1350. track 1780 1686/1620	1455/1424	
Wheelbase mm	2550	4285	2870
Track contact mm	2835	2020	1250
Track width mm	240	320	300
Ground clearance mm	wheels 290/tracks 360	300	235
Length-width-height	5010-2160-2000	6530-2010-3000	4550-2000-2320
Maximum weight kg	5600	10,000	5420
Payload kg	2500	to 6000	1000
Seats	8-10	2-3	1-9
Fuel consumption			38
Fuel capacity l/100 km			
Performance: climbs	30%	50%	59%
Wades mm			
Spans mm			
Notes			

light towing 1-ton	light towing 1-ton	light towing 1-ton	light towing 3-ton
Sd.Kfz. 10	Sd.Kfz. 10	HK. 601	HK. 600
D 6	D 7 HK 601	HL kl 3	
Demag	Demag, Adler, Saurer, Buessing-NAG	Demag	Hansa Lloyd Goliath
1937-1938	1938-1944	1940-1942	1936
D 672/1 of 12/2/1940	D 672.5 of 8/8/1940	WaA Handbook D9	Borgward data
Maybach NL 38 TRKM	Maybach HL 42 TRKM	Maybach HL 45 Z	Hansa-Lloyd L 3500 L
6 in-line	6 in-line	6 in-line	6 in-line
90 x 100	90 x 110	95 x 110	82 x 110
3791	4199	4678	3485
6.6 : 1	6.6 : 1	6.7 : 1	6 : 1
2400	2800	3800	3200
83	100	147	71
dropped	dropped	dropped	dropped
8 journal	8 journal	8 journal	4 journal
1 Solex 40 JFF II	1 Solex 40 JFF II	1 Solex 40 JFF II	1 Solex 40 BHF
1-5-3-6-2-4	1-5-3-6-2-4	1-5-3-6-2-4	1-5-3-6-2-4
Bosch BJH 1.4/12	Bosch EJD 1.8/12	Bosch EJD 1.8/12	Bosch GJ
Bosch RKC 130	Bosch RKCN 300	Bosch RKCN 300	Bosch RJG
1/12/94	1/12/94	1/12/75	1/12/90
Solex pumps after Maybach drawing 224534/1			pump
water	water	water	water
Dry multiplate	2-plate PF 20 K	dry 1-plate	dry 1-plate
Demag-Adler	Maybach Variorex	Maybach Variorex	Hansa-Lloyd-Goliath
6/1	7/3 8/3	4/1 x 2	
tracks, front	tracks, front	tracks, front	tracks, front
---			1 : 9.8
50	65	65	50
230/130	S = 285/G = 150*		
	rigid axle		rigid axle
ZF Cletrac hydraulic	ZF Cletrac mechanical	ZF Ross	Spindle
9.0	9.0	10.0	
Transverse leaf springs/transverse torsion bars same			
High-pressure & central			high-pressure
A. Teves	A. Teves	A. Teves	Deutsche Perrot
Hydraulic	hydraulic	hydraulic	mechanical
Inner drum	inner drum	inner drum	inner drum
Drive wheels	drive wheels	drive wheels	drive wheels
Steering brakes	steering brakes	steering brakes	steering brakes
Sheet steel disc	sheet steel disc	sheet steel disc	sheet steel disc
6.00 Tr-20	6-00 Tr-20**	190-18	6.50-20
1630/1580	1630/1580	1700/1620	1400/1300
2430	2430	2680	
1470	1470	1800	1200
240	240	280	280
325	325	350	350
4271-1824-1750	4750-1840-1620	5545-2100-2000	4900-1730-1950
3850	499	6300	5000
1200	1500	2800	1450
8	8	9	2-6
40	40	S =45/G = 75	
110	110		100
24 degrees	24 degrees	24 degrees	24 degrees
---			---
700	700		500
1500	1500		---

* S = road, G = off-road; ** road wheels 550 x 45-479

Vehicle			
Type	Light towing 3-ton	light towing 3-ton	off-road truck
Maker	HL kl 5	HL kl 6	Daimler-Benz [?]
	Borgward	Borgward, Hanomag, Adler, Horch, Skoda	Daimler-Benz
Years built	1937-1938	1938-1945	1937-1938
Data source	Borgward data	D 660/2 of 8/1/1943	Daimler-Benz archive
Motor Type	Hansa-L-G L 3500 L	Maybach HL 42*	Daimler-Benz M 18
Cylinders	6 in-line	6 in-line	6 in-line
Bore x stroke mm	82 x 110	90 x 100	78 x 100
Displacement cc	3485	4170	2867
Compression ratio	6 : 1	6.7 : 1	6.5 : 1
RPM	3200	2800	3650
Horsepower	71	100	68
Valves	dropped	dropped	standing
Crankshaft bearings	4 journal	8 journal	7 journal
Carburetor	1 Solex 40 BFH	1 Solex 40 JFF II	1 Solex 35 BFVLS
Firing order	1-5-3-6-2-4	1-5-3-6-2-4	1-5-3-6-2-4
Starter	Bosch GJ	Bosch EJD 1.8/12	Bosch BIH 1.4/12
Generator	Bosch RJG	Bosch RKCN 300	Bosch RIG 90
Batteries	1 12-volt 90 Ah	1 12-volt 75 Ah	2 6-volt
Fuel feed	pump	Solex pump	pump
Cooling	water	water	water
Clutch	dry 1-plate	dry 1-plate F&S	dry multiplate
Gearbox	Hansa-Lloyd-Goliath	Hanomag U 50	ZF Aphon
Gears forwd/reverse	4/1 x 2	4/1 x 2	4/1 x 2
Drive wheels	tracks, front	tracks, front	tracks, front
Axle ratio	1 : 9.8	1 : 9.8	
Top speed kph	53	52.5	45
Range km road/off	275/150	240.140	
Front axle	rigid	rigid	rigid
Steering	spindle	Hanomag spindle or Ross worm gear	Screw spindle
Turning circle	13.5 m	13.5 m	9.5 m
Springs front/rear	transverse leaf/ Torsion bars	transverse leaf/ torsion bars	longit. Semi-ellipt./ semi-ellip. & coil
Chassis lubrication	high-pressure	high-pressure	central
Brake system			
Manufacturer	Deutsche Perrot	Deutsche Perrot	ATE & Daimler-Benz
Effect	mechanical	mechanical/comp. air	hydraulic
Brake type	inner drum	inner drum	inner drum
Footbrake works on	drive wheels	drive wheels	front & drive wheels
Handbrake works on	steering brakes	steering brakes	drive wheels
Wheel type	sheet steel disc	sheet steel disc	sheet steel disc
Tires front/rear	7.25-20	7.25-20 or 190-18	5.50-15
Track front-rear mm	1650/1600	1650/1600	1340/1180
Wheelbase mm	2730	2780	2600-2675
Track contact mm	1800	1800	700
Track width mm	280	280	290
Ground clearance mm	320	320	220
Length-width-height	5550-2000-215	5550-2000-2150	6280-1600
Maximum weight kg	7000	7200	3450
Payload kg	1550	1800	800
Seats	7 + 1	7 + 1	2-3
Fuel consumption	S = 45/G = 75 l/100 km	S = 40/G = 80 l	62 l/100 km
Fuel capacity	100 liters	110 liters	
Performance: climbs	24 degrees	24 degrees	---
Climbs mm			---
Wades mm	500	500	---
Spans mm			---
Notes		* First series: Maybach HL 38	

Artillery Tractor	medium towing	medium towing	medium towing
HBT	2-ton	5-ton	5-ton
	Sd.Kfz. 6	Sd.Kfz. 6	Sd.Kfz. 6
	BN I 5	BN I 7	BN I 8
AB Volvo	Buessing-NAG	Buessing-NAG, DB	Buessing-NAG, DB
1942-1943	1935	1936-1937	1938-1939
Volvo data	D 606/4, 4/1/1938	D 606/4, 4/1/1938	D 606/7, 6.7.1939
Volvo FC	Maybach NL 35 Spl.	Maybach NL 38 TR	Maybach NL 38 TUK
6th series	6th series	6th series	6th series
92.07 x 110	90 x 90	90 x 100	90 x 100
4400	3435	3791	3791
5.25 : 1	5.6 : 1	6.7 : 1	6.6 : 1
3000	3000	3000	3000
90	90	100	100
dropped	dropped	dropped	dropped
7 journal	8 journal	8 journal	8 journal
1 Solex	1 Solex	1 Solex	1 Solex 40 JFF II
1-5-3-6-2-4	1-5-3-6-2-4	1-5-3-6-2-4	1-5-3-6-2-4
Bosch EJD 1.4/12	Bosch BJH 1.4/12	Bosch BJH 1.4/12	Bosch BJH 1.4/12
Bosch RJH 90/12	Bosch RKC 130.12	Bosch RKC 130/12	Bosch RKC 130/12
1/12/70	1/12/75	1/12/75	1/12/75
Pump	pump	pump	pump
Water	water	water	water
Dry 1-plate	dry 2-plate	dry 2-plate F & S PF 220 K	dry 2-plate F & S PF 220 K
Volvo DB	ZF pre-selector	ZF pre-selector	ZF pre-selector
4/1 x 2	4/1 x 2	4/1 x 2	4/1 x 2
tracks, front	tracks, front	tracks, front	tracks, front
1 : 5.31	S = 1.0, G = 160 [?]	S = 1.0, G = 3.3	S = 1.0, G = 3.3
65	50	50	50
	S = 320/G = 160	250	300
Rigid axle	rigid axle	rigid axle	rigid axle
	Worm gear	work & Cletrac	Muenz S 3.5 worm
9.0	13.0		13.0
Transverse leaf, torsion bars	transverse half-leaf, longitudinal half-leaf	transverse half-leaf, longitudinal half-leaf	transverse leaf, torsion bars
High-pressure	high-pressure	high-pressure	high-pressure
Lockheed	Deutsche Perrot	Deutsche Perrot	Bosch and Perrot
Hydraulic	mechanical/comp.air	mechan., comp.air	mechan., comp.air
Inner drum	outer band	inner drum	inner drum
Drive axle	drive wheels	drive wheels	drive wheels
Drive axle	steering brakes	steering brakes	steering brakes
Pierced sheet steel	sheet steel disc	sheet steel disc	sheet steel disc
7.00-20	7.50-20	7.50-20	210-18
1660/1620	1825/1700	1825/1700	1825/1700
	3360	3360	3200
	1270	1270	2025
	320	320	320
325	400	400	400
5680-2000-6555	6020-2000-2500	6020-200-2500	6115-260-2270
1800	8800	8800	8500
2 + 8	1500	1500	1500
115	15 or 10	15 or 10	15 or 10
	50	50	60
	120 + 40 = 160	120 + 40 = 160	165 + 20 = 185
	24 degrees	24 degrees	24 degrees

700	600	600	600

		---	

	medium towing 5-ton Sd.Kfz. 6	heavy Wehrmachts-schlepper	tracked truck 2-ton (Maultier, Sd.Kfz. 3)
Vehicle			
Type	BN 9	sWS	2t MT V 3000 S/SSM
Maker	Buessing-NAG,Praga	Buessing-NAG,Tatra	Ford-Werke AG
Years built	1939-1943	1943-1945	1942-1944
Data source	D 606/11, 2/29/1940	D 606/15. 12/5/1943	D 666/409, 7/26/1943
Motor type	Maybach HL 54 TURKM	Maybach HL 42 TRKMS	Ford G 39T or G 19T
Cylinders	6 in-line	6 in-line	V8
Bore x stroke mm	100 x 115	90 x 110	80.95 x 95.25
Displacement cc	5420	4198	3924
Compression ratio	6.7 : 1	6.6 : 1	5.9 : 1
RPM	2600	3000	3500
Horsepower	115	100	95
Valves	dropped	dropped	standing
Crankshaft bearings	8 journal	8 journal	3 journal
Carburetor	2 Solex 40 JFF II	1 Solex 40 JFF II	1 Solex 30 FF JK
Firing order	1-5-3-6-2-4	1-5-3-6-2-4	1-3-6-2-7-8-4-5
Starter	Bosch BJH 1.8/12	Bosch EJD 1.8/12	Bosch BIH 1,4/12
Generator	Bosch RKC 130/12	Bosch RJJK 130/12	Bosch RJH 130/12
Batteries/volts/Ah	1/12/75	1/12/75	1/12/50
Fuel feed	pump	pump	Solex punp PE 1453
Cooling	water	water	water
Clutch	F & S PF 220 K dry two-plate	Ford dry 1-plate	Ford pre-selector
Gearbox	ZF pre-selector	ZF kb 40 D	
Speeds fwd./reverse	4/1 x 2	4/1 x 2	5/1
Drive wheels	tracks, front	tracks, front	tracks, front
Axle ratio	S = 1.0/G = 3.3	1 : 4.11	1 : 6.66
Top speed kph	50	27.4	39.6
Range km	S = 300, G = 115	S = 300, G = 100	S = 200, G = 75
Front axle	rigid	rigid	rigid
Steering	ZF Ross 660 worm	Cletrac	Ford worm gear
Turning circle m	15.0	15.0	19.0
Springs front/rear	transverse leaf+ Torsion bars	transverse leaf + torsion bars	longitudinal half + coil springs
Chassis lubrication	high-pressure	high-pressure	central,*
Brake system	ATE & Perrot	Argus	ATE & Ford
Effect	mechan./comp.air	suction	hydraulic
Brake type	inner drums	discs	inner drums
Footbrake works on	drive wheels	drive wheels	wheels & run. Gear
Handbrake works on	steering brakes	steering brakes	steering brakes
Wheel type	sheet steel discs	sheet steel discs	sheet steel discs
Tires front/rear	210-18	270-20	190-20 or 7.25-20
Track front/rear mm	1825/1700	2100/1950	1650/1790
Wheelbase mm	3275	3475	
Track contact mm	2200	2040	1840
Track width mm	320	500	260
Ground clearance mm	360	465	270
Length-width-height	6325-260-2500	6675-2500-2830	6325-2245-2773
Maximum weight kg	9000	13,500	5860
Payload kg	1500	4000	2000
Seats	15 or 10	2 + 10	2-3
Fuel consumption	S = 60, G = 160 l	S = 80, G = to 300	S = 55, G = 40
Fuel capacity l	190	240	110
Performance: climbs	24 degrees	24 degrees	20 degrees
Climbs mm		---	
Wades mm	600	1000	440
Spans mm	2000	---	

Notes   * high-pressure from Chassis no. 547304 on

Tracked truck 2-ton (Maultier, Sd.Kfz. 3)	tracked truck 2-ton Opel run. Gear proto.	tracked truck 2-ton (Maultier Sd.Kfz. 3)	tracked truck 2-ton (Maultier)
S 3000/SS M	2 t 3.6-36 S/M	2 t 3.6/36 S/SS M	L 4500 R
Kloeckner-Humb.Dtz.	Adam Opel AG	Adam Opel AG	Daimler-Benz AG
1942-1944	1942-1943	1942-1943	1943-1944
D 666/407, 7/26/1943	Opel data 10/10/1942	D 669/419, 7/26/1943	D 667/403, 10/27/43
KHD F 4 M 513	Opel 3.6 liter	Opel 3.6 liter	DB OM 67/4
4th series	6th series	6th series	6th series
110 x 130	90 x 95	90 x 95	105 x 140
4942	3626	3626	7274
22 : 1	6 : 1	6 : 1	20 : 1
250	3120	3120	2250
80	68	68	112
dropped	dropped	dropped	dropped
3 journal	4 journal	4 journal	7 journal
Diesel Bosch PE 4B	1 Solex 35 JFP	1 Solex 35 JFP	Diesel Bosch PE 6*
1-3-4-2	1-5-3-6-2-4	1-5-3-6-2-4	1-5-3-6-2-4
Bosch BNG 4/24	Bosch CJ 1.2/12	Bosch CJ 1.2/12	Bosch BNG 4/24
Bosch RKCK 300/12	Bosch RKC 130/12	Bosch RKC 130/12	Bosch RKCK 300/12
2/12/94.5	1/12/50 or 62	1/12/50 or 62	2/12/105
pump	pump	pump	pump
water	water	water	water
F&S 1-plate dry	one-plate dry	one-plate dry	F&S 1-plate dry
ZF Faks 40	Opel pre-selector	Opel pre-selector	DB Fak 45 (ZF lic.)
5/1	5/1	5/1	5/1 x 2
tracks, front	tracks, front	tracks, front	tracks, front
1 : 6.8	1 : 6.5	1 : 6.38	1 : 9.2
40	38	38	36
S = 170/G = 80	S = 165/G = 100	S = 220/G = 100	S = 220/G = 100
Rigid	rigid	rigid	rigid
ZF Ross Type 700	worm gear-roller	worm gear-roller	ZF Ross Type 72
19.0	12.8	15.0	16.8-22.0
long. leaf + coil	longitudinal leaf	long.half + coil	long. half +quarter
central	high-pressure	high-pressure	central
A. Teves	A. Teves	A. Teves	ATE-Lockheed-Knorr
Hydraulic	hydraulic	hydraulic	hydr. compr.air
Inner drum	inner drum	inner drum	inner drum
Wheels & runn.gear	wheels & runn.gear	wheels & runn.gear	wheels & runn.gear
Steering brakes	steering brakes	steering brakes	steering brakes
Sheet steel disc	sheet steel disc	sheet steel disc	sheet steel disc
190-20	190-20	190-20	270-20
1640.1780	1542/1790	1542/1790	1860/1800
	3108		1825
1840	1665	1840	2400
260	260	260	300
250	265	265	360
6120-222220-2800	6010-2340-2960	6000-2280-2710	7860-2360-3215
6650	6600	5930	12700
2000	2650	2000	4500
2-3	2-3	2-3	2-3
S = 28.5/G = 70	S = 40-45/G = 90	S = 40-45/G = 90	S = 60/G to 140
70	92 + 20 = 112	82	140
	70%	24 degrees	
	---	440	
700	900		

	---		

*or Deckel-PSA

Vehicle	med. towing 8-ton (Sd.Kfz. 7)	med. towing 8-ton (Sd.Kfz. 7)	med. towing 8-ton (Sd.Kfz. 7)
Type	KM m 8	KM m 9	KM m 10
Maker	Krauss-Maffei, DB, Buessing	Krauss-Maffei	Krauss-Maffei, Borgward
Years built	1934-1935	1935-1936	1936-1937
Data source	D 607/3, 11/1/1935	D 6-7/8. 11/24/1938	D 607/8, 11/24/1938
Motor type	Maybach HL 52 TU	Maybach HL 57 TU	Maybach HL 62 TUK
Cylinders	6 in-line	6 in-line	6 in-line
Bore x stroke mm	100 x 110	100 x 120	105 x 120
Displacement cc	5184	5698	6191
Compression ratio	6.3 : 1	5.6 : 1	6.5 : 1
RPM	2600	2600	2600
Horsepower	115	130	140
Valves	dropped	dropped	dropped
Crankshaft bearings	8 journal	8 journal	8 journal
Carburetor	2 Solex 40 MMOVS	1 Solex 40 JFF II	1 Solex 40 JFF II
Firing order	1-5-3-6-2-4	1-5-3-6-2-4	1-5-3-6-2-4
Starter	Bosch BNF 2.5/12	Bosch BNF 2.5/12	Bosch BNG 2.5/12
Generator	Bosch RKC 130/12	Bosch RKC 130/12	Bosch RJJK 130/12
Batteries/volts/Ah	1/12/105	1/12/105	1/12/105
Fuel feed	Pallas CV pump	Pallas C 9 W pump	Pallas C 9 W pump
Cooling	water	water	water
Clutch	F & S dry 2-plate	Mecano K 230 K dry two-plate	Mecano K 230 K dry two-plate
Gearbox	ZF ZG 55	ZF Aphon G 55	ZF Aphon G 55
Speeds fwd./reverse	4/1 x 2	4/1 x 2	4/1 x 2
Drive wheels	tracks, front	tracks, front	tracks, front
Axle ratio	1 : 5.25	1 : 5.42	1 : 5.42
Top speed KPH	50	50	50
Range km	250	290	290
Front axle	rigid	rigid	rigid
Steering	worm gear	ZF Ross worm gear	ZF Ross worm gear*
Turning circle m	14.0	14.0	14.0
Springs front/rear	Transverse leaf, longitudinal semi-elliptic leaf		
Chassis lubrication	high-pressure	high-pressure	high-pressure
Brake system	Deutsche Perrot/Bosch	Deutsche Perrot/Bosch	Deutsche Perrot/Bosch
Effect	compressed air	compressed air	compressed air
Footbrake works on	drive wheels	drive wheels	drive wheels
Handbrake works on	steering brakes	steering brakes	steering brakes
Wheel type	cast steel spoked	cast steel spoked	cast steel spoked
Tires front/rear	32 x 6 or 7.50-20	32 x 6 or 7.50-20	32 x 6 or 7.50-20
Track front/rear mm	1940.1750	1940/1750	1940/1750
Wheelbase mm	---	---	---
Track contact mm	1400	1400	1400
Track width mm	360	360	360
Ground clearance mm	410	410	410
Length-width-height	6690-2350-2760	7175-2350-2500	7175-2350-2500
Maximum weight kg	11,000	10,740	10,740
Payload kg	1500	1800	1800
Seats	11	11	11
Fuel consumption l	70 l/100 km	S = 80/G = 200	S = ? /G = 200
Fuel capacity l	100 + 100 = 200	135 + 70 = 205	135 + 70 = 205
Performance: climbs	24 degrees	24 degrees	24 degrees
Climbs mm	---		
Wades mm	650	650	650
Spans mm	---		
Notes	*or Muenz Type 4		

Med. towing 8-tom (Sd.Kfz. 7)	med. towing 8-ton	towing wgn. 10-ton	heavy towing 12-ton (Sd.Kfz. 8)
KM m 11	61	ZD 5	DB s 7
Krauss-Maffei,*	Breda SA	Daimler-Benz AG	Daimler-Benz AG
1938-1945	1944	1931-1932	1934-1935
D 6-7/5, 10/9/1939	D 605/13, 1944 ed.	Daimler-Benz archives	D 608/2, 2/1/1940
Maybach HL 62 TUK	Breda T 14	Maybach DSO 8	Maybach DSO 8
6 in-line	6 in-line	V-12 60 degrees	V-12 60 degrees
105 x 120	110 x 130	92 x 100	92 x 100
6191	7412	7973	7973
6.5 : 1	5 : 1	6.3 : 1	6.3 : 1
2600	2400	2300	2300
140	130	150	150
dropped	dropped	dropped	dropped
8 journal	7 journal	8 journal	8 journal
1 Solex 40 JFF II	2 Zenith 42 TTPVS	2 Solex 35 MOV	2 Solex 35 MOV
1-5-3-6-2-4	1-5-3-6-2-4	1-12-5-8-3-10-6-7-2-11-4-9	1-12-5-8-3-10-6-7-2-11-4-9
Bosch BNG 2.5/12	Bosch BNG 4/24	Bosch BNE 2/12	Bosch BNE 2/12
Bosch RJJK 130/12	Bosch CQLN 300/24	Bosch TDV 6 400/12	Bosch
1/12/105	2/12/105	1/12/100	2/12/105
Pallas pump	pump	2 electric pumps	pump
Water	water	water	water
Mecano dry 2-plate	dry 2-plate	Long dry 2-plate	Mecano dry 2-plate
ZF pre-selector	ZF pre-selector	Maybach DSC 110	DB pre-selector
4/1 x 2	5/1 x 2	5/1	4/1 x 2
tracks, front	tracks, front	tracks, rear	tracks, front
1 : 5.42		1 : 3.9	S = 1.0/G = 1.771
50	50	38	50
S = 250/G = 135	270-300		
Rigid	rigid	swing axle	rigid
Muenz worm gear	worm gear	screw with Cletrac	ZF Ross worm gear
16.0	16.0	10.6	
half trans.& long.	half trans. & long.	conical springs	leaf trans. & long.
high-pressure	high-pressure	high-pressure	high-pressure
Bosch/Perrot	Marelli	Knorr/DB	Knorr
Mech., comp. air	compressed air	compressed air	compressed air
Inner drum	inner drum	inner drum	inner drum, outer band
Drive wheels	drive wheels	drive wheels	drive wheels
Steering brakes	steering brakes	steering brakes	steering brakes
Cast steel spoked	cast steel spoked	sheet steel pierced	cast steel spoked
9.75-20	9.75-20	150 x 670	9.00-20
2000/1800	2020/1800	2000/1800	1900/1850
3470	3470	---	---
2235	257	1870	2150
360	360	350	400
400	390	340	400
6850-2400-2620	6900-2450-2750	6245-2360-2350	6800-2350-2200
11550	13000	9300	14400
1800	1800		1800
11	11	1 + 11	12
S = 80/G = 200	70		S = 100/G = 220
175+38=213, later**	170 + 35 = 205	175 + 25 = 200	
24 degrees	24 degrees	12 degrees	12 degrees

650	800		---
1800	1800		

*Borgward, Saurer, **165+38=203

Vehicle	heavy towing 12-ton (Sd.Kfz. 8)	heavy towing 12-ton (Sd.Kfz. 8)	heavy towing 12-ton (Sd.Kfz. 8)
Type	DB s 8	DB 9	DB 10
Maker	Daimler-Benz AG	Daimler-Benz AG	Daimler-Benz, Krupp
Years built	1935-1938	1938-1939	1939-1944
Data source	D 608/2, 2/1/1940	D 608/7. 11/27/1939	D 608/11, 1/12/1940
Motor type	Maybach DSO 8	Maybach HL 85 TUKRM	Maybach HL 85 TUKRM
Cylinders	V-12 60 degree	V-12 60 degree	V-12 60 degree
Bore/stroke mm	92 x 100	95 x 100	95 x 100
Displacement cc	7973	8520	8520
Compression ratio	6.3 : 1	6.2 : 1	6.5 : 1
RPM	2300	2500	2500
Horsepower	150	150	185
Valves	dropped	dropped	dropped
Crankshaft bearings	8 journal	8 journal	8 journal
Carburetor	2 Solex 35 MOV	2 Solex 40 JFF II	2 Solex 40 JFF II
Firing order	1-12-5-8-3-10-6-7-2-11-4-9	1-12-5-8-3-10-6-7-2-11-4-9	1-12-5-8-3-10-6-7-2-11-4-9
Starter	Bosch BNE 2/12	Bosch BNG 4/24	Bosch BNG 4-24
Generator	Bosch	Bosch GQL 300/12	Bosch GQL 300/12
Batteries/volts/Ah	2/12/105	2/12/105	2/12/105
Fuel feed	pump	pump	pump
Cooling	water	water	water
Clutch	Mecano dry 2-plate	F & S dry 2-plate	F & S dry 2-plate
Gearbox	DB pre-selector	ZF Allklauen-	ZF Spl. pre-selector
Gears fwd/reverse	4/1 x 2	4/1 x 2	4/1 x 2
Drive wheels	tracks, front	tracks, front	tracks, front
Axle ratio	S = 1.0/G = 1.771	S = 1.0/G = 1.771	S = 1.0/G = 1.771
Top speed kph	50	51	51
Range km		250	S = 250/G = 125
Front axle	rigid	rigid	rigid
Steering	ZF Ross worm gear	worm gear	ZF Ross worm gear
Turning circle m	21.0	21.0	21.0
Springs front/rear	leaf/torsion bars trans.	leaf/torsion bars trans	leaf/torsion bars trans
Chassis lubrication	high-pressure	high-pressure	high-pressure
Brake system			
Manufacturer	Knorr/DB	Knorr/DB	Knorr/DB
Effect	compressed air	compressed air	compressed air
Brake type	inner drum	inner drum	inner drum
Footbrake works on	drive wheels	drive wheels	drive wheels
Handbrake works on	steering brakes	steering brakes	steering brakes
Wheel type	cast steel spoked	cast steel spoked	cast steel spoked
Tires front.rear	11.25-20	11.25-20	11.25-20
Track front/rear	1900/1900	1900/1900	2010/1900
Wheelbase mm	3670	3670	3670
Track contact mm	2500	2500	2500
Track width mm	400	400	400
Ground clearance mm	400	400	400
Length-width-height	7100-2400-2800	7100-2400-2800	7350-2500-2770
Maximum weight kg	15000	15000	14700
Payload kg	1600	1600	2550
Seats	1/3 [13?]	13	13
Fuel consumption l	S = 100/G = 220	S = 100/G = 250	S = 100/G = 250
Fuel capacity l	210 + 40 = 250	210 + 40 = 250	210 + 40 = 250
Performance: climbs	24 degrees	24 degrees	24 degrees
Climbs mm			
Wades mm	630	630	630
Spans mm	2000	2000	2000
Notes			

heavy towing wagon (HK. 1601)	heavy towing 18-ton (Sd.Kfz. 9)	heavy towing 18-ton (Sd.Kfz. 9)	heavy towing 18-ton (Sd.Kfz. 9)
HK. 1601/1604	FM gr 1	F 2	F 3
Daimler-Benz, Famo	Famo	Famo	Famo, Vomag, Tatra
1941-1942	1936-1937	1938	1939-1944
Handb.WaA Blatt D	Handbuch WaA	D 671/1, 3/4/1943	D 671/1, 3/4/1943
Maybach HL 116 Z	Maybach HL 98 TUK	Maybach HL 98 TUK	Maybach HL 108
6 in-line	V-12 60-degree	V-12 60-degree	V-12 60-degree
125 x 150	95 x 115	95 x 115	100 x 115
11048	9780	9780	10838
6.5 : 1	6.5 : 1	6.5 : 1	6.5 : 1
3300	2600	3000	3000
265	20	250	270
dropped	dropped	dropped	dropped
8 journal	7 roller	7 roller	7 roller
2 Solex 40 JFF II	2 Solex 40 JFF II	2 Solex 40 JFF II	2 Solex 40 JFF II
4-4-4-4-4-4	1-8-5-10-3-7-6-11-2-9-4-12	1-8-5-10-3-7-6-11-2-9-4-12	1-8-5-10-3-7-6-11-2-9-4-12
Bosch BNG 4/24	Bosch BNG 4/24	Bosch BNG 4/24	Bosch BNG 4/24
Bosch GQL 300/12	Bosch GQL 300/12	Bosch RKC 130/12	Bosch BNG 4/24
2/12/105	2/12/105	1/12/105	1/12/105
pump	2 pumps	2 pumps	2 pumps
water	water	water	water
dry 2-plate	dry 2-plate	F & S dry 2-plate	F & S dry 2-plate
ZF Spl. pre-selector	ZF Aphon	ZF G 65 VL 230	ZF G 65 VL 230
6/1	4/1 x 2	4/1 x 2	4/1 x 2
tracks, front	tracks, front	tracks, front	tracks, front
		1 : 1.96	1 : 1.96
67.5	50	50	50
	280	S = 260/G = 100	S = 260/G = 100
rigid	rigid	rigid	rigid
hydr. worm gear	worm gear	ZF Ross Model 760 worm gear	ZF Ross Model 760 worm gear
	21.6	21.6	21.6
leaf/torsion bar trans	leaf/torsion bar trans	leaf/torsion bar trans	leaf/torsion bar trans
high-pressure	high-pressure	high-pressure	high-pressure
Knorr/Daimler-Benz	Bosch/Westinghouse	Bosch	Bosch
Compressed air	compressed air	compressed air	compressed air
Inner drums	inner drums	inner drums	inner drums
Drive wheels	drive wheels	drive wheels	drive wheels
steering brakes	steering brakes	steering brakes	steering brakes
cast steel spoked	cast steel spoked	cast steel spoked	cast steel spoked
11.25-20	12.75-20	12.75-20, road wheels 900/80-80	
2030/2000	2100/2000	2100/2000	2100/2000
4030	4015	4015	4060
2600	2860	2860	2860
400	440	440	440
400	440	440	440
7770-2600-2350	7700-2600-2650	8250-2600-2850	8320-2600-2850
16200	18000	18000	18000
	2000	2620	2620
depends on body	depends on body	depends on body	depends on body
	S = 100/G = 300	S = 120/G = 310	S = 120/G = 310
		230 + 60 = 290	230 + 60 = 290
	24 degrees	24 degrees	24 degrees

		800	800
			2500

	small tracked cycle (Sd.Kfz. 2)	0.6/1-ton towing	1.6-ton towing
Vehicle		M 36	prototype
Type	HK 101	ADMK	ADAT
Maker	NSU, Stoewer	Steyr-Daimler-Puch	Steyr-Daimler-Puch
Years built	1940-1945	1935-1938	1937
Data source	D 624/1, 10/28/1942	Data, Vienna 1938	Steyr data
Motor type	Opel 1.5 liter	AD FB 12/20	AD M 640
Cylinders	4 in-line	4 in-line	6 in-line
Bore/stroke mm	80 x 74	80 x 115	85 x 115
Displacement cc	1488	2312.2	3915.4
Compression ratio	6 : 1	4.25 : 1	5.77 : 1
RPM	3400	1400	3000
Horsepower	36	20	80
Valves	dropped	standing	dropped
Crankshaft bearings	4 journal	3 ball	7 journal
Carburetor	1 Solex 32 FJ II	1 Pallas MP 30	1 Zenith 48 VI
Firing order	1-3-4-2	1-3-4-2	1-5-3-6-2-4
Starter	Bosch EGD 0.6/6	none	Scintilla 12 V
Generator	Bosch REDK 75/1	Scintilla	Scintilla 12 V/100 W
Batteries/volts.Ah	1/6/75	none	1/12/60
Fuel feed	gravity + pump	AC PE 626 pump	pump
Cooling	water	air, fan	water
Clutch	dry 1-plate	semi-wet 2-plate	dry 2-plate
Gearbox	NSU pre-selector	AD Type 440	AD Type ADAT
Speeds fwd/reverse	3/1 x 2	4/1	4/1
Drive wheels	tracks, front	rear	rear
Axle ratio	1 : 4.09	1 : 5.56	
Top speed kph	80	45 on wheels	70 on wheels
Range km	250	S = 200/G = 110	
Front axle	socket axle	swing axle	swing axle
Steering	Cletrac	screw	worm gear
Turning circle m	4.0	8.4	
Springs front/rear	fork, coil/torsion bar	half-leaf, transverse	half-leaf transv/longit.
Chassis lubrication	high-pressure	high-pressure	central
Brake system			
Manufacturer	NSU	Austro-Daimler	ATE-Lockheed
Effect	mechanical	mechanical	hydraulic
Brake type	inner drum	inner drum	inner drum
Footbrake works on	drive wheels	rear wheels	rear wheels
Handbrake works on	steering brakes	rear wheels	drive
Wheel type	sheet steel disc	sheet steel disc	sheet steel disc
Tires front/rear	3.50-19Kr 4611	5.25-18	230-18
Track front/rear mm	-/816	1290 (870 full-track)	1365/1800 (1310 full)
Wheelbase mm	1352	1770	3200
Track contact mm	820	1260	
Track width mm	170	190 (swamp 340)	
Ground clearance mm	230	270	
Length-width-height	3000-1000-1200	3570-1500-1300	5280-2030-1735
Maximum weight kg	1560	2040	
Payload	325	600	1600
Seats	3	3	9
Fuel consumption l	16-22	S = 17/G = 35	30
Fuel capacity l	42		37
Performance: climbs	24 degrees	45 degrees	
Climbs mm		300	
Wades mm	440	600	
Spans mm		1800	
Notes			

1.5/2-ton towing	light towing U (f)	light towing 37 (f)	Towing wagon S (f)
M 37 off-road	ZgKw U 305 (f)	ZgKw U 304 (f)	Zgkw S 307 (f)
AFR	TU 1	P 107	MCG
Austrian Auto (OAF)	Unic, Geo. Richard	Unic, Geo. Richard	SOMUA
1936	1939-1943	1937-1939	1932-1935
OAF data	D 628/3. 1/7/1942	D 628/1, 5/20/1941	D 628/6, 3/4/1942
OAF AFN-S	Unic M 16 D	Unic P 39	Somua
4 in-line	4 in-line	4 in-line	4 in-line
98 x 125	80 x 107	100 x 110	100 x 150
3800	2150	3450	4712
4.8 : 1	5.5 : 1	5.5 : 1	5.6 : 1
2400	3200	2800	2000
75	50	60	60
dropped	dropped	dropped	dropped inlet, standg.exhaust
3 journal	3 journal	5 journal	3 journal
1 Zenith T 36	1 Solex 35 RFNY	1 Solex 35 RTNB	1 Solex 40 RFNV
1-2-4-3	1-2-4-3	1-3-4-2	1-3-4-2
Bosch CJ 1.2/12	12 volt	6 or 12 volt	DS 2 BS or by hand
Light battery ignition	12 volt	Citroen 6 or 12 volt	GS 2/12 volt
1/12/60	1/12/57	2/6 or 1/12/90	2/6/92
pump	SEV 4 K pump	pump	pump
water	water	water	water
dry one-plate	dry one-plate	dry one-plate	dry one-plate
AF pre-selector	Unic B 169 synchro.	Unic synchronized	geared wheel
4.5.8 or 10/1-2	4/1 x 2	4/1 x 2	5/1
tracks, front	tracks, front	tracks, front	tracks, front
	1 : 0.1994	1 : 2.9 or 3.2	1 : 3.5
45	50	45	36
	250	400	170
rigid	rigid	rigid	rigid
worm gear-spindle			
12.0			
half leaf longitudinal	leaf longitudinal	half leaf longitudinal	half leaf longitudinal
high-pressure	high-pressure	high-pressure	high-pressure
ATE-Lockheed	Unic	Unic	Somua
Hydraulic	mechanical	hydraulic	mechanical
Inner drum	inner drum	inner drum	outer band
Both axles	front+drive wheels	drive wheels	gearbox
Gearbox	front+drive wheels	drive wheels	drive wheels
Sheet steel disc	sheet steel disc	sheet steel disc	sheet steel disc
7.00-20 or 7.00-18	5.25-18		30 x 5
1440	1277/1200	1395/1340	1485/1480
2750			
	1400	2500	
385	175	260	
220	310	340	
? –1966-2600	4200-1500-1310	4850-1800-2280	5350-1880-2750
5100	2910	5400	7300
2000	475	1400	2000
2-3 or by body	to 10	5	2-3
30-50	S = 28/G = 50	S = 40/G = 100	47
75	80	160	80
60 degrees			
600	500	800	

Vehicle	light armored wagon (Sd.Kfz. 250)	medium armored w. (Sd.Kfz. 251)	light armored ammunition tr. Sd.Kfz. 252
Type	D 7 p	H kl 6 p	D 7 p
Maker	Demag, others	Weserhuette, others	Demag
Years built	1940-1945	1937-1945	1940-1941
Data source	D 672/5, 8/8/1940	D 660/4, 5/15/1943	D 672/5, 8/8/1940
Motor type	Maybach HL 42 TRKM	Maybach HL 42 TRKM	Maybach HL 42 TRKM
Cylinders	6 in-line	6 in-line	6 in-line
Bore/stroke mm	90 x 110	90 x 110	90 x 110
Displacement cc	4171	4171	4171
Compression ratio	6.7 : 1	6.7 : 1	6.7 : 1
RPM	2800	2800	2800
Horsepower	100	100	100
Valves	dropped	dropped	dropped
Crankshaft bearings	8 journal	8 journal	8 journal
Carburetor	1 Solex 40 JFF II	1 Solex 40 JFF II	1 Solex 40 JFF II
Firing order	1-5-3-6-2-4	1-5-3-6-2-4	1-5-3-6-2-4
Starter	Bosch EDJ 1.8/12	Bosch EDJ 1.8/12	Bosch EDJ 1.8/12
Generator	Bosch RKCN 300/12-1300	Bosch RKCN 300/12-1300	Bosch RKCN 300/12-1300
Batteries/volts/Ah	1/12/94	2/12/75	1/12/94
Fuel feed	pump	pump	pump
Cooling	water	water	water
Clutch		F & S Mecano PF 220 K dry two-plate	
Gearbox	Maybach Variorex	Hanomag 021-32785	Maybach Variorex
Gears fwd./reverse	7/3	4/1 x 2	7/3
Drive wheels	tracks, front	tracks, front	tracks, front
Axle ratio		1 : 2.06	
Top speed kph	65	52.5	65
Range km	S = 320/G = 200	S = 300/G = 150	S = 350/G = 175
Front axle	rigid	rigid	rigid
Steering	worm gear	Hanomag or ZF Ross	worm gear
Turning circle m	9.0	11.0	9.0
Springsfront/rear	leaf/torsion b. transv.	half transv/torsion b.	leaf/torsion b. transv.
Chassis lubrication	high-pressure	high-pressure	high-pressure
Brake system			
Manufacturer	ATE/Perrot	Perrot Type 440x80	ATE/Perrot
Effect	hydraulic	compr. air/suction	hydraulic
Brake type	inner drum	inner drum	inner drum
Footbrake works on	drive wheels	drive wheels	drive wheels
Handbrake works on	steering brakes	steering brakes	steering brakes
Wheel type	sheet steel disc	sheet steel disc	sheet steel disc
Tires front/rear	6.00-20	7.25-20 or 190-18	6.00-20
Track front/rear mm	1630/1580	1650/1600	1630/1580
Wheelbase mm	2500	2775	2500
Track contact mm	1020	1800	1020
Track width mm	240	280	240
Ground clearance mm	285	320	285
Length-width-height	4560-1945-1660	5800-2100-1750	4700-1950-1800
Maximum weight kg	5800	9000	5730
Payload kg	800	1500	1000
Seats	depends on use	depends on use	2
Fuel consumption l	S = 40/G = 80	S = 40/G = 80	S = 40/G = 80
Fuel capacity l	140	160	140
Armor front mm	14.5	14.5	14.5
Armor side mm	8	8	8
Armor rear	8	8	8
Performance: climbs	24 degrees	24 degrees	24 degrees
Climbs mm	---		
Wades mm	700	500	700
Spans mm	1900	2000	1900
Notes			

Vehicle	lt. arm. observation Wagon (Sd.Kfz. 253)	lt. arm. towing wagon	lt. arm. towing wagon
Type	D 7 p	HKp 602/603	HKp 606
Maker	Wegmann	Demag	Demag
Years built	1940-1941	1940-1942	1941-1942
Data source	D 672/5, 8/8/1940	Handbuch WaA 10	Handbuch WaA
Motor	Maybach HL 42 TRKM	Maybach HL 45 Z	Maybach HL 50
Cylinders	6 in-line	6 in-line	6 in-line
Bore/stroke mm	90 x 110	95 x 110	100 x 106
Displacement cc	4171	4678	4995
Compression ratio	6.7 : 1	6.7 : 1	6.7 : 1
RPM	2800	3800	4000
Horsepower	100	147	180
Valves	dropped	dropped	dropped
Crankshaft bearings	8 journal	8 journal	8 journal
Carburetor	1 Solex 40 JFF II	1 Solex 40 JFF II	1 Solex
Firing order	1-5-3-6-2-4	1-5-3-6-2-4	1-5-3-6-2-4
Starter	Bosch EJD 1.8/12	Bosch EJD 1.8/12	Bosch
Generator	Bosch RKCN 300 12-1300	Bosch RKCN 300 12-1300	Bosch
Batteries/volts/Ah	1/12/94	2/12/75	2/12/75
Fuel feed	pump	pump	pump
Cooling	water	water	water
Clutch	Mecano dry 2-plate	dry two-plate	dry two-plate
Gearbox	Maybach Variorex	Maybach-Hanomag	Maybach OLVAR
Speeds fwd./reverse	7/3	8/3	8/3
Drive wheels	tracks, front	tracks, front	tracks, front
Axle ratio	---		
Top speed kph	65	75	70
Range km	S = 350/G = 175		
Front axle	rigid	rigid	single wheel
Steering	worm gear	ZF Ross hydraulic	ZF Ross
Turning circle m	9.0		
Springs front/rear	leaf/torsion b.transv.	leaf/torsion b.transv.	leaf/torsion b.transv.
Chassis lubrication	high-pressure	high-pressure	high-pressure
Brake system	ATE/Perrot	Deutsche Perrot	Sueddeutsche. Perrot
Effect	hydraulic	suction	suction
Brake type	inner drum	inner drum	disc
Footbrake works on	drive wheels	drive wheels	drive wheels
Handbrake works on	steering brakes	steering brakes	steering brakes
Wheel type	sheet steel disc	sheet steel disc	sheet steel disc
Tires front/rear	6.00-20	190-18	190-18
Track front/rear mm	1630/1580	1700/1620	1700/1650
Wheelbase mm	2500	2680	2600
Track contact mm	1020	2680 [?]	1500
Track width mm	240	280	280
Ground clearance mm	285	350	350
Length-width-height	4700-1950-1800	5545-2100-1730	4850-1980-1850
Maximum weight kg	5700	8000	7000
Payload kg	690	1240	1000
Seats	4	12	8
Fuel consumption l	S = 40/G = 80		
Fuel capacity l	140		
Armor front mm	14.5	14.5	14.5
Side mm	8	8	8
Rear mm	8	8	8
Performance: climbs	24 degrees	24 degrees	24 degrees
Climbs mm	400		
Wades mm	700		
Spans mm	1500		
Notes			

Bibliography

Boelke, Willi A., *Deutschlands Ruestung im Zweiten Weltkrieg*
Feist, Uwe, *German Halftracks in Action*
------, *Schuetzenpanzer in Action*
Guderian, Heinz, *Erinnerungen eines Soldaten*
Icks, Robert J., *Talks and Armored Vehicles*
Magnuski, Janusz, *Wozy Bojowe*
Mellenthin, F. W. von, *Panzer Battles*
Munzel, Oskar, *Die deutschen gepanzerten Truppen bis 1945*
Nehring, Walther K., *Die Geschichte der deutschen Panzerwaffe 1916-1945*
Ogorkiewicz, R. M., *Armour*
Oswald, Werner, *Kraftfahtzeuge und Panzer der Reichswehr, Wehrmacht und Bundeswehr*
Schausberger, Norbert, *Ruestung in Oesterreich 1939-1945*
Scheibert, H. & C. Wagener, *Die deutsche Panzertruppe 1939-1945*
Senger und Etterlin, F. M. von, *Die deutschen Panzer 1926-1945*
Spielberger, Walter J., *Profile: Sd. Kfz. 251*
Spielberger, Walter J. & Uwe Feist, *Armor Series*
Stoves, Rolf, *Die 1. Panzer Division*
Vanderveen, Bart H., *Observer's Fighting Vehicle Directory*

As well as:

Bellona Handbook No. 2, Part 1-3, compiled by Peter Chamberlain and Hilary L. Doyle

Common Abbreviations

A/A	old type, old version
A (2)	infantry unit of the War Ministry
A (4)	field artillery unit of the War Ministry
A (5)	foot artillery unit of the War Ministry
A 7 V	transport unit of the War Ministry
AD (2)	General War Dept., Section 2 (infantry)
AD (4)	General War Dept., Section 4 (field artillery)
AD 5	General War Dept., Section 5 (foot artillery)
AHA/Ag K	General Army Office, Motor Vehicle Group
AK	Artillery Design Bureau
AKK	Army vehicle column
AlkW	Army truck
ALZ	Army freight train
AOK	Army High Command
APK	Artillery Testing Commission
ARW	eight-wheel vehicle
A-Typen	with all-wheel drive (fast type)
BAK	anti-balloon gun
Bekraft	fuel dept., field vehicle office
BMW	Bavarian Motor Works
Chefkraft	Chief of field vehicle office
(DB)	Daimler-Benz
DMG	Daimler Motor company
Dtschr.Krprz.	German Crown Prince
E-Fahrgestell	uniform chassis
E-Pkw	uniform personnel car
E-Lkw	uniform truck

Fa	field artillery
FAMO	Fahrzeug- und Motorenbau GmbH
Fgst	chassis
FF-Kabel	field phone cable
FH	field howitzer
FK	field cannon
Flak	anti-aircraft gun
F.T.	radio/telegraph
Fu	radio
Fu Ger	radio set
Fu Spr Ger	radio speaker
g	secret
Gen. St. d. H.	Army General Staff
Gengas	generator gas
G. I. d. MV.	Inspector-general of Motor Vehicles
g. Kdos.	Secret command matter
gp	armored
g. RS	secret Reich matter
gl	off-road capable
GPD	Gun Testing Commission
Gw	gun vehicle
(H)	rear engine
Hanomag	Hannoversche Maschinenbau AG
HK	halftrack
H.Techn.V.Bl.	Army technical information sheet
HWA	Army Weapons Office
I.D.	infantry division
I.G.	infantry gun
In.	inspection
In. 6	inspection of motor vehicles
Ikraft	inspection of field vehicles
ILuk	inspection of air and ground vehicles
K	cannon, (big) gun
K	small
KD	Krupp-Daimler
K.D.	cavalry division
KdF	Kraft durch Freude (Nazi organization)
K.d.K.	Commander of Mobile Troops
K.Flak	motorized anti-aircraft gun
Kfz.	Motor vehicle
KM	Ministry of War

KP	motorized limber
(Kp)	Krupp
Kogenluft	Commanding General of Air Forces
Krad	Motorcycle
Kr.Zgm.	motorized towing machine
KS	fuel injection
Kw	motor vehicle, combat vehicle
KrKW	ambulance
KOM	motor bus
KwK	tank gun
l	light
L/	caliber length
le	light
le FH	light howitzer
le FK	light field gun
l. F. H.	light howitzer
le. I. G.	light infantry gun (also l.I.G.)
le. W. S.	light Wehrmacht tractor
LHB	Linke-Hoffman-Busch
Lkw	truck
LWS	land-water tractor

[column 2]

m	medium
MAN	Maschinenfabrik Augsburg-Nuernberg
MG	machine gun
MP	machine pistol
MTW	crew transport vehicle
Mun.Pz.	armored ammunition carrier
n	revolutions per minute
n/A	new type, new version
NAG	Nationale Automobilgesellschaft
(o)	stock, on the civilian market
Ob.d.H.	Commander of the Army
O. H. L.	Army High Leadership
O. K. H.	Army High Command
O. K. W.	Wehrmacht High Command
Pak	antitank gun
P. D.	armored division
Pf	engineer vehicle
Pakw	personnel vehicle
Pz. F.	armored ferry

Pz. Kpfwg.		tank
Pz. Spwg.		armored scout car
Pz. Jg.		tank destroyer
Pz. Bef. Wg.		armored command car
(R)	on tracks. Tracked	
R/R		wheel/track-driven
(RhB)		Rheinmetall-Borsig
RS		tracked tractor
RSG		mountain tractor
RSO		Raupenschlepper Ost (tractor)
RV		aiming communication [?]
Sankra		medical corps vehicle
s		heavy
sFH		heavy howitzer
schg.		able to run on rails
Schlp.		tractor
schf.		amphibious
Sd.Anh.		special trailer
Sd.Kfz.		special vehicle
Sfl.		self-propelled gun mount
Sf		self-propelled
S-Typen		fast rear-drive vehicles
SmK		pointed shell with core

SPW	armored personnel (rifle)vehicle
SSW	Siemens-Schuckert-Werke
s. W. s.	heavy Wehrmacht tractor
StuG	assault gun
StuH	assault howitzer
StuK	assault cannon
Tak	antitank gun
Takraft	Technical Dept, Inspection of Vehicles
TF	radio frequency
Tp	tropical version
Vakraft	Test Dept, Motor Vehicles (WWI), Test Dept., Inspection of Motor Vehicles (*Reichswehr* and *Wehrmacht*)
ve	fully disarmed
v.max	maximum velocity
V^0	muzzle velocity
VPK	Traffic Testing Commission
Vs.Kfz.	test vehicle
VKz	test vehicle
ZF	Zahnradfabrik Friedrichshafen
ZRW	ten-wheeled vehicle
Zgkw	towing vehicle
WaPruef/WaPrw	Vehicle Testing Office
Wumba	Weapon and Ammunition Procurement Office
wg	amphibious, able to go in water

THE SPIELBERGER GERMAN ARMOR AND MILITARY VEHICLE SERIES

Armored Vehicles

OF THE GERMAN ARMY 1905-1945

WH-71172

Walter J. Spielberger

A SCHIFFER MILITARY HISTORY BOOK

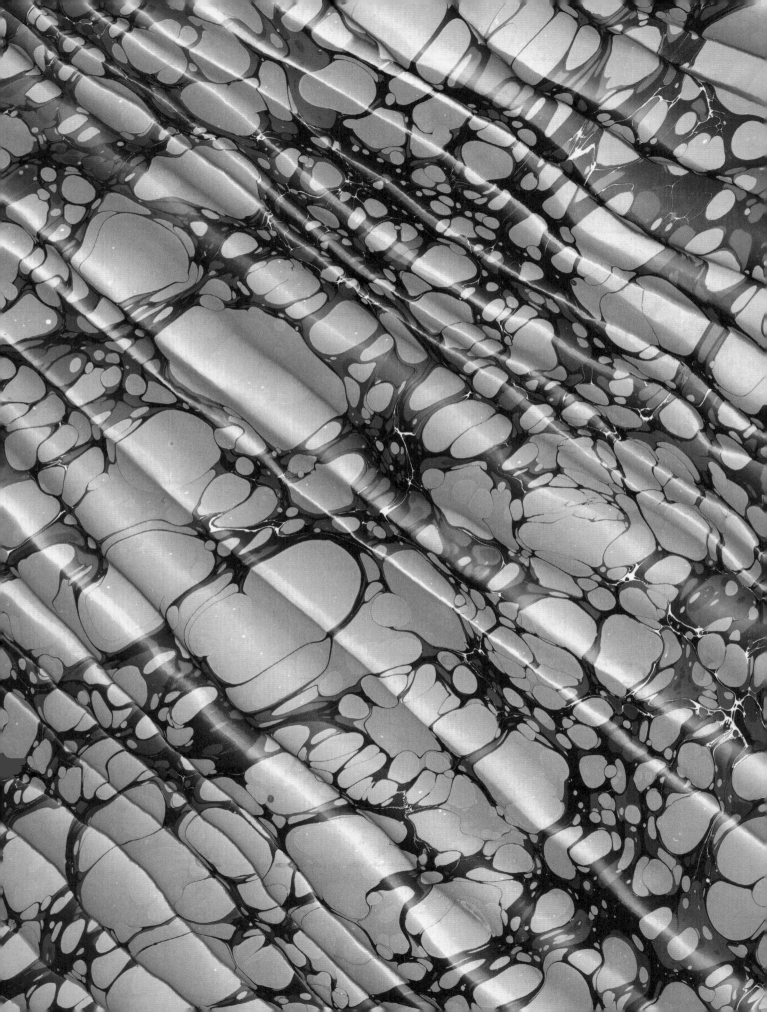